PUBLIC S
PRIVATE GRIEF

Hele & Lies

24   48
      24
    8 2

The extraordinary life of an angel investor, cancer patient and dad

PETER COWLEY AND LIESBETH BLOM

Published by Invested Investor Limited

This is edition one, in 2024

www.publicsuccess-privategrief.com

For privacy reasons, some names, locations, and dates may have been changed. This book does not replace the advice of a medical professional. The book is based on Peter Cowley's memories, from his perspective.

Cover designed by Rolando Ugolini. Typesetting by Natalie White.

Front cover photos © Peter Cowley

ISBN 978-1-9164079-8-5 (paperback)

ISBN 978-1-9164079-9-2 (ebook)

Dedicated to the memory of Ian/Nam and Alan,
who died far too young.

This book deals with the themes of alcoholism, cancer, mental health and suicide. More information for support, resources and charities can be found in the 'Weblinks for reference' section at the end of the book.

Love Is:

Love lights up a darkened space,
Love opens up your soul's desire,
Love is often o'so rare,
Yet especially Love is all that's there.

Love cannot be bought,
Yet it can be given to no end.
Love cannot be taken,
Yet if you ask for it, you shall receive.

Love is Light and Joy and Warmth.
To remember where we came from,
Is to return home, never alone.
For we are all one, glued with love.

Ian Cowley

Contents

Preface

This book was first thought of after the death of my youngest son Alan, in late 2022. I had produced two books before, *The Invested Investor* and *Founder to Founder*, which were written with the help of local author Kate Kirk and with Alan himself, who was instrumental in self-publishing them. After Alan's death, I realised that perhaps there was a more personal book in me, one about the dramatic ups and downs in my life. I'd come across the saying that 'everyone has a book in them, but in most cases that's where it should stay', but I felt I had things to say that might inspire or help others.

I started in May 2023 by writing 1,200 words about my middle son Ian's death in 2009. Liesbeth was only marginally involved at this stage, being unsure how she could help and feeling that she might be too close to me for a collaboration to work. However, together, we drafted a draft book proposal to send to prospective publishers and agents to get them interested. I had spent many years reviewing thousands of investment pitch decks, and a book proposal is similar, except it is in prose rather than a slide deck. The proposal went through a dozen versions as we got feedback from friends and contacts in the publishing industry.

As part of the proposal, Liesbeth wrote a sample chapter from our experiences of Christmas 2021 when I was told I had cancer, but not which type of cancer. We then shared the proposal and sample chapter with a dozen agents and publishers and received useful feedback. Still, none would take the book unless they could read it in full or see that I had over 100,000 social media followers (I have about a tenth of that), so we decided to follow the self-publishing route. In any case it is very likely it would have taken a year longer with a publisher than to self-publish, and there is a good chance that I may not have that long left (Liesbeth disagrees!). Getting to grips with self-publishing was a bit of a learning curve, since much of the knowledge that had been built up in self-publishing died with Alan.

The book has been researched from my memories, from diaries (both personal and calendars) that I have kept for all my adult life, from family photos dating back to the 1930s, and by talking to family and friends. As the project progressed, we fell into a mode of working where I produced the raw text and Liesbeth turned this raw text, with its business English and bullet points, into prose. In our many discussions, which could sometimes be painful, we were able to dig more deeply into some of my experiences, adding more personal material. She also wrote some of the chapters (1, 5, 16 and 17) based on my scribblings, notes, dictations, and podcast transcripts and structured the material so that the story is (hopefully) easy to follow.

To keep the production process simple and affordable, we decided to put photographs on the associated website, rather than embed them in the book. The 'Reflections' chapter is also reproduced on the website.

It should be emphasised that we all experience life through different lenses, with different perspectives, and also that our memories get modified over time, commonly for self-protection. Readers who have known me for some or nearly all of my life may have different recollections of the interactions described and we apologise if something has been misremembered. Please do let us know, as we hope to publish a second edition with additions and corrections.

And finally, if only a few people are inspired by this book and make changes to their lives, we will feel the effort expended by us and many others will be worthwhile. In my data-driven way, in the summer of 2023, I decided on the number 600.

I thought that it would take us about 600 hours to write the book, and hence if one person reads the book per hour that we have expended, we will have reached 'breakeven'. I have spent many hundreds of hours mentoring entrepreneurs and angel investors on a one-to-one basis and have equated these numbers.

We hope that this book will inspire others to cope with the ups and downs that we all experience in our lives and that you will feel it was worth your time reading this book.

Peter Cowley
Liesbeth Blom

Cambridge
February 2024

Acknowledgements

Many people have helped us write this book, some in a very immediate way, and many others – too many to mention by name – by simply listening, encouraging and showing their interest. We thank you all.

The following friends and colleagues encouraged me from the very start and helped us develop the book proposal and our ideas around its structure once we started work on it together: Amelia Thorpe, Kate Kirk, Janine Hornsby, Selma Prodanovic, Tim Mills, Jonathan Brech, David Gill, Victor and Sarah Christou, Chris Smith, Luther Philips, Jo Whitehead, Jon Bradford, Anna Jagric, Katy Tuncer and Pilgrim Beart – we are so grateful for your support and input. We would also like to thank Andrew Hewitt and Brian Harris, who were our immensely helpful and insightful first readers, Lisa Edwards of Redwood Tree Publishing for her incisive and invaluable feedback as our development editor, Catherine Blom-Smith for her perceptive feedback on the first draft and for her meticulous copyediting and proofreading work later in the process, and Natalie White for her careful typesetting. Our thanks also go to Faye, Carole and Gemma of Cofinitive Communications, who went above and beyond in carrying out their highly effective marketing, design and PR work, and to Keith Heppell for the cover photography.

We are very grateful to Maggi, Pete, Martin, Paula, Ged and Katherine for their sensitive and pertinent comments on the wordings used in the alcoholism, cancer and suicide chapters, and to my oncologist David for checking the information around EGFR+ lung cancer and the descriptions of my cancer care so far. Any errors or omissions that remain are entirely our responsibility and we would gratefully receive any feedback to that effect, so that we can correct any errors in a later edition.

Many thanks to my close friends Emma Belgrove and Dawn Walker, as well as my sister-in-law Susie Cowley for helping to fill in memory gaps from several decades ago.

Over a hundred of my friends and colleagues are mentioned in the book who helped make me the man I am today, but I would like to give a special mention to those who believed in me before I believed in myself: Greg Meekings, Lothar Ulbrich, Georg Pyttel, Richard Kavaliauskas, Robert Sansom, Robert Marshall, Tim Mills and Candace Johnson.

We would both like to thank our families for their love, support and patient encouragement throughout the project.

Chapter 1

In the Consultant's Office

Addenbrooke's Hospital, Cambridge

30 December 2021

I'm sitting in the waiting room of our local hospital, with my girlfriend Liesbeth next to me. We talk quietly, wondering what awaits us inside the respiratory consultant's room. I have my laptop with me – one of the startups where I am on the board as an investor director is going through a rocky time and needs my support. Liesbeth, always more 'in the moment' than me, is looking around at the other people waiting – what could be wrong with them? – at the receptionist behind her plastic screen checking people in, the pin-board on the wall, still decorated with some tinsel. I look through some figures and check in by email with the CEO of the startup in rocky waters.

The previous three weeks had been by turns confusing and frightening, as we moved back and forth between appointments with a GP and various neurologists, and now we are waiting for the big reveal. We are waiting to find out the results of my latest test and we have absolutely no idea what to expect.

In the couple of months leading up to Christmas I had started to notice problems with my balance. I nearly fell off my bicycle several times and found myself reaching out for furniture to steady myself around the house. Nonetheless, I hadn't really thought much of it. With hindsight, perhaps I was showing the typical behaviour of a man ignoring signs of ill health.

At the time, I was isolating with Covid and so assumed the problem was related to that. However, there was another small issue on which I wanted some medical advice, so I made a video appointment with a private GP. While I was talking to him, it seemed a good idea just to mention my balance. I wondered aloud to him whether it could be related to Covid, but he had not heard of it as a symptom. He suggested I came in to see him in person, which I did. I told him what had been going on and then he said: "Could you walk across the room, please?" I stood up. "Heel to toe," he specified. Like a tightrope walker... but as soon as I lifted my foot off the floor, I felt I was going to fall over. The GP put out a hand to steady me. We were both surprised – in fact, he seemed shocked – that I couldn't take a single step in this way without his hand to keep me from tipping over.

He sent me away with the recommendation that I should see a neurologist as soon as possible. At this point he seemed far more worried than I was. I still did not think much of it, but I took his advice and tried to find a neurologist to take a look at me. This proved very difficult – the first available appointment was many weeks away. When I told my GP this, he made some phone calls and managed to find a neurologist in our local private hospital who could fit me in just a few days later. Looking back, his sense of urgency should have worried me – I still hadn't grasped how seriously the GP was taking the situation.

The weekend intervened and that particular weekend I was going skiing with friends. I am a full-time angel investor, investing in technology startups, helping these fledgling businesses to grow through mentoring and support. I am heavily involved in a local group of angel investors called the Cambridge Angels, and it was with some of these colleagues and friends that I travelled to the resort of Les Arcs in the French Alps for a weekend on the slopes.

We arrived at the resort and I got out of the hire car. Glancing around me as I stepped out of the car, I saw nothing but snow, which suddenly seemed quite daunting. As I took the first tentative step, I found that I could not keep my balance; I could not really walk on the snow safely. There was no way I was going to be able to ski. Just two months earlier I had run the Cambridge Half Marathon, and I was still doing 5k runs almost every other day, but walking slowly – or walking on snow – was now very difficult. So, I spent the weekend reading and working while watching the others out on the slopes through the window of our apartment. I felt somewhat sorry for myself but was still able to enjoy the surroundings and the company of my friends in the evenings.

I was seen by the neurologist on the Tuesday after we returned. He ran some tests similar to those in the GP's surgery, making me walk heel to toe, asking me to follow his finger waving in the air and to touch my nose with my index finger, then sent me back to the waiting room.

A little while later he came out to tell us that he was flummoxed. Flummoxed. A strange word for a highly trained and experienced neurologist to use, direct but not exactly encouraging. He had expected me to have other symptoms. Still, we didn't panic. He thought it would be a good idea to get an MRI scan that same day, in the same (private) hospital, but this turned out to be impossible. However, they could fit me in on Friday, a week or so before Christmas.

Off I went on Friday, to go through the slightly unpleasant experience of lying in a very noisy tunnel while the machine did its work. When I'd had an MRI done previously in my life, I'd been given a disc with the images straight away, so I asked for my disc this time, too. "Oh sorry, the DVD writer is broken," was the answer of one radiographer, followed by a quick "and we don't have any discs anyway," by another. This strange coincidence should have set some alarm bells ringing, but instead I shrugged and went on my way.

Around 7pm that evening, Liesbeth and I were just about to go out when the phone rang. It was the neurologist from the hospital, who asked me if I had someone with me. He told me I had four tumours in my brain, the largest of which measured 17mm across and was pressing on my cerebellum, causing the balance problem. We were completely stunned. All the pieces from the previous week very quickly fell into place as we realised how the GP and the neurologists had been protecting me – the GP by fast tracking me and the radiographers by not letting me see the images of my brain, all while trying to get a quick diagnosis, a diagnosis that they had clearly foreseen and feared all along. The scales well and truly fell from our eyes at that moment, as we stood in the kitchen with our coats on, while he went on to explain gently that they thought these tumours in the brain were secondary tumours. What did this mean? What would lie ahead of me? I now know that people do also get benign brain tumours, but at that moment, all I thought was: my life is in danger, and meanwhile my quality of life will be heavily compromised. What can be done? What can I do?

As we were trying to process this devastating news, the neurologist continued talking us through what he wanted to happen. He proposed that I start taking corticosteroids straightaway, since these would reduce the swelling around the tumours and so help with my symptoms. They would buy some time while the medics did more tests and discussed the best way forward.

The phone call ended, and we were left trying to digest everything he had said. What would they find? How would we tell my children what was happening? When would the GP get the steroid prescription to us? Where could we get hold of a pharmacy over the weekend? Were we still going out this evening? All these thoughts whirled through our heads. It is pretty frightening to be told there is something wrong with your brain. Most of us fear not only losing control over our lives, but losing ourselves, our identity. To think there are tumours growing inside your head – the centre of your sense of self – is very scary.

At the same time, I didn't panic. Yes, being told I had a tumour in my brain was a shock, but not cause for panic. Instead, we became very practical and started to look up where we could get the much-needed steroids and try to understand what these tumours could mean.

I did what everyone around me and my own common sense told me not to do: I started to google. There was really no point, because many cancers have brain tumours as 'secondaries' (where cancer cells break away from the primary tumour and settle and grow in another part of the body). But I am not good with uncertainty, and I was trying to find out as much as possible. The only slight relief it gave me was the realisation that if the brain tumours *were* secondaries, then it clearly wasn't brain cancer. That was relatively good news, since brain cancer is much harder to treat, at least that is what Dr Google told me. I have since disciplined myself to only look things up on Google when there is a very specific question, treatment or drug to research. Otherwise, you end up going down myriad rabbit holes, each one even scarier (and more irrelevant) than the one before.

At this point, both of my remaining children, Matt, the eldest, and Alan, the youngest, were away. Matt had been living outside the UK for the past two decades, working all over the world to support his climbing, sailing, hiking and other adventurous pursuits. At that time, he was in Mallorca. Meanwhile, Alan and his wife were skiing in Austria. I set up a Zoom call with the five of us and told them what we knew so far.

Matt was very quiet and serious. His first comment was: "Lots of work to do." He is like me in some ways in that he cuts to the chase immediately: this is the reality, these are the hard facts, now how are we going to deal with this? Alan, a much gentler soul, was clearly strongly affected. "We love you, Dad, we are here for you, we will support you. Shall we come home straightaway?" Of course I told them to enjoy their holiday and not come back early. There was nothing anyone could do, until we had a great deal more information. Yes, it was all very worrying, but I was eager to find out more and to know what the next stages were.

A period of waiting started. Waiting for a CT scan, waiting to hear the result, waiting to find out the prognosis and what kind of treatment might be available. At the neurologist's suggestion, I had been handed over to the NHS by this point and two days before Christmas, the CT scan was done. By the evening, we were told that they could see a shadow on my right lung. Cancer. Up to that point, the word cancer had not been used, but now, it seemed this was the world I was about to enter.

When I was growing up, the C-word was regarded pretty much as a death sentence. I had experienced this first-hand when my younger brother died of leukaemia in 1980, aged just twenty-one. I have read about cancer and seen it many times since, both at a distance in friends and acquaintances, and close up in loved ones, who had to go through unpleasant chemo treatments and worse. Part of me had always believed that I would get cancer at some point in my life, as a result of the alcoholism I had suffered with for many years before finally getting dry and becoming what is called a recovering alcoholic, with help from Alcoholics Anonymous. I had not had an alcoholic drink for over twenty-one years, but I knew about the undeniable link between alcoholism and the increased risk of getting any kind of cancer.

We went into Christmas in a daze. Since my divorce and the death of my middle son, Christmas had not been my favourite time of year, as is the case for many people who have suffered a devastating loss. Given half a chance, I tried to be far away, out of the country, somewhere else in the world doing something I enjoyed. It was clearly not going to happen that year. The next appointment was scheduled for the 30th of December and so

I was looking at a very long week of waiting, watching people celebrate, trying to be a reasonable presence at Christmas dinner tables and by Christmas trees.

By Christmas itself, both of my sons were back in the UK. I spent some time with Alan and his wife's family in a house full of children and dogs and great food, which was a good distraction. I also spent some time in Liesbeth's flat. Her divorce was different from mine, and she was used to celebrating Christmas not just with her two daughters, but also with her ex-husband, who would usually spend the day with them. It was quite a squeeze in her tiny flat, and it was not necessarily easy to have the festivities going on around me, however sensitively, while I sat quietly in my chair, but it was good to be with kind people.

Thanks to the steroids, my balance had improved, and I was able to move around more easily. Unfortunately, high doses of steroids have side-effects that are tricky for the person taking them, and can be pretty difficult, too, for the people around them. I had trouble sleeping and spent many hours awake at night, sitting at my desk in front of spreadsheets, planning. Having lost weight successfully in the previous two years, I now ate everything in sight and put quite a lot of weight back on. I am told I became quite agitated and irritable in my behaviour to Liesbeth and others in my immediate environment. However, the steroids were doing their job of keeping the swellings around the tumours down for the time being.

✳   ✳   ✳   ✳   ✳

It is the eve of New Year's Eve, and we are in the waiting room at our hospital, about to see a respiratory consultant to talk us through the CT results in more detail. This is the moment we've been waiting for all week. Facts, information, answers of some sort. I trained as a computer scientist in the early days of computing, and data is my stock-in-trade. The first company I ever founded, and which has been the source of so much of the knowledge and experience that I now share, lecture and publish on all over the world, is based around data. Numbers are my friends (although I am lucky enough to have plenty of human ones, too); they are how I approach the world, how I make sense of the world. I have a spreadsheet with my health data going back over twenty years and have always thought of myself as a cyberchondriac (where you start to imagine you have all sorts of diseases from looking on the internet too much), or one of the 'worried well' (someone who is unnecessarily anxious about their physical or mental health). Now I am about to be given some of the most important data I will ever receive about the state of my body.

When we go in, there are two people in the room: the respiratory specialist and someone who turns out to be a member of the specialist cancer nurse team for lung cancers. Once we sit down, the specialist explains he will talk us through the CT scan results and then discuss options. We are seated in such a way that we can see the screen for ourselves.

The first screen shows the shadow on the right lung that we have already been told about. Radiologists are really the only people who can read scans properly, and it is not easy for laypeople to make out a great deal on the black and white images on a computer screen, taken from an unfamiliar angle, but we can clearly see what he is pointing at as the tumour in the lung. Long thin arms are streaking out from that tumour to other parts of my lung. Then he pulls up the next screen. "This is the shadow on the liver – can you see over here?" We can. Then he pulls up the next screen. "There are also tumours in your ribs, this white area here." Another screen. "I'm afraid we have also found these." He points at an adrenal gland, which clearly shows the same ugly shadow.

Then the next screen comes up. "These are the lymph nodes, and there are some tumours there." We are reduced to stunned silence. What we are seeing is my upper body positively riddled with tumours. So many, in so many places. Stage IV, which means it is very advanced and has metastasised a long way from the original lung tumour.

How can anyone survive this for long?

I am shell-shocked.

As I sit there, reeling, the consultant continues to talk, as clearly and as kindly as he can, but I struggle to take in what he is saying. Fortunately, Liesbeth is taking notes.

He says they need to do a biopsy, to determine the genetic make-up of the cancer. This gives them information about the particular cancer mutation in my body, which will influence the choice of treatment. Liesbeth keeps asking questions and the consultant lists a number of possible mutations and treatments. We arrange an appointment for the biopsy, which will be taken very soon indeed. Then, ever the realist, I ask if I should put my affairs in order. He replies that there are treatments, and they are going to try and help me, but that yes, this is probably a good idea.

We leave the room in shock. The cancer nurse takes us to another room, offering to make cups of tea and answer any more questions, but really, we just want to leave, to be by ourselves and try to digest what has just happened – and more importantly, decide what we are going to do with that information. It has been only thirteen days since the preliminary diagnosis.

It feels like a lifetime.

Chapter 2
The Dentist's Son from Hull

I was born in 1955, in Hull. Dad was a dentist, or a dental surgeon as he liked to call himself, running a practice with his two younger brothers. They'd taken over this practice from their father, who had set it up in the 1930s. Mum, although she'd studied Pharmacy, was mainly a housewife. She was the elder of two sisters born in Burnley, Lancashire, and when she was young, her family had moved to Hull, living in the same building as the public baths which her father ran. My father was brought up in Hull, and apart from evacuation during the war and studying dentistry in Leeds, he lived in and around Hull most of his life. Although the dental practice seemed to work well until the late 1970s, I do remember him saying "a partnership is a sinking ship," presumably referring to the stresses between the three brothers.

When I was two, my brother David was born. We moved from a flat to a semi-detached house with a large garden in a road called Newland Park, a leafy suburb close to Hull University, where many academics and the famous poet Philip Larkin lived, and which was described by Larkin's university colleague John Kenyon as 'an entirely middle-class backwater'. This pretty much sums up where I grew up. My sister Susan was born four years after we moved to Newland Park.

We had a traditional upbringing, with Mum running the home as well as doing the accounts for the dental practice.

In her spare time, she seemed to me to be very content with embroidery, watching TV and relaxing. We had a live-in au pair for a while when I was about nine years old, who introduced me to The Beatles. However, the au pair didn't seem to work out as far as my parents were concerned. Were they worried about a rebellious influence? She left soon after and if it had been an experiment for my parents, it was one that was not repeated. We had a similar experience with a gorgeous cocker spaniel puppy, who was with us for only a year. I was not yet ten years old at the time, but I was disappointed by the loss of both, as they brought some novelty into a somewhat dull household.

Dad was very sociable and Mum was happy to entertain, so we spent many weekends getting together with friends of theirs, mostly dentists and their spouses, as well as seeing our cousins locally. The family environment felt homely and comfortable, with family meals and family trips, and watching TV together. Dad also spent a lot of time in the garden tending flowers and large fruit and vegetable patches. To this day, I don't like gardening, probably because I tend to need intellectual challenge, but also because I am impatient and it takes a long time between making a change to a garden and seeing the result – except, of course, for cutting the grass!

My parents rubbed along together well enough, although I never saw any affection between them. I've never been sure whether this was simply how their generation behaved, or whether it was particular to their relationship. Mum would infrequently get very angry. Once, she left a friend's house where we were visiting and drove off in the car by herself to return two hours later. Another time she threw a piece of crockery at Dad and a piece of the pot got stuck in the plaster. These incidents both happened in my early teens, and I had no idea at the time what lay behind her anger. It could have been due to frustration about her unfulfilled career or issues within the marriage. Perhaps it was her health; she was bedridden at one point with rheumatoid arthritis. Thirty years later, when they were both in their eighties and Mum was ill, I went to visit and was alarmed to find Dad in tears, saying she was "so difficult to live with," but this was when she was really struggling with her health, mostly house-bound and wanting to die.

From when I was quite young, the family used to have a three-week holiday abroad in the summer, and occasional holidays during the rest of the year in the UK. The summer holidays were initially in hotels in Switzerland and Austria. One of my earliest memories is of the Vitznauerhof Hotel on Lake Lucerne, when David and I – five and seven years old respectively – left our hotel room and walked down to the main restaurant where our parents were trying to have a quiet meal together, to the other guests' amusement. We were having a brotherly tiff and once this was sorted out, we were packed off back to bed. Later on, my parents bought a caravan and we used to take this around Europe, including Spain, France, the Alps, and what was then Yugoslavia. I was very lucky to have exposure to other cultures, people, and scenery from an early age. This formed the foundation of the sense of curiosity and exploration that has defined my life, including visiting nearly ninety countries to date. During the rest of the summer, the caravan was left near Scarborough in North Yorkshire. Mum and us three children would stay there and my father used to commute back to Hull to work during the week.

While I was revising for my A levels, we took what I was told was the first fly-drive holiday by a British family to the USA, driving a motorhome from New York to Miami. I had recently passed my driving test, so was allowed to drive. New York was amazing and scarily busy and crowded, and in Florida I remember picking oranges directly from trees at our campsite. David and I slept in a tent and the motor home toilet leaked – what an adventure!

My brother, David, was very different from me. He was practical, sociable and not really academic. We had a close relationship as teenagers, although there were the usual teenage tensions. He had to pass through my bedroom to get to his, which is not an ideal arrangement at that age. David was sixteen when I left home to go to university, so we saw much less of each other. Our time together was more or less restricted to my long university vacations, when I used to help him restore his old Austin 1100 and we would occasionally go clubbing.

On these clubbing nights, he had a tendency to play pranks on our way home. One of his favourites was to call random people from a payphone at three in the morning (in those days, all calls within Hull were free). I was uncomfortable with him doing this, but at the same time I didn't do anything to stop him. I looked up to him in some ways, because I was a bit geeky, very geeky, actually, and academic, while he was just a 'normal' person. David didn't go on to the sixth form and was working at a model paint company, Humbrol, when he met his future wife, Susie. I was sad to see him leave the UK, aged twenty, to go and live with Susie's family in New Zealand – it was such a long way away. He was diagnosed with leukaemia while in New Zealand and immediately returned to the UK together with Susie, by then his fiancée, and I was very happy he was back, despite his illness. He was treated for nine months, during which time they got married and I was the best man. It was a devastating blow to the family, and my first encounter with death, when he passed away six weeks after his last treatment, aged just twenty-one.

My sister, Sue, was six-and-a-half years younger than me, and like David, she was bright but not academic. She left school, going to work in the showjumping industry as a groom for twenty years. She worked her way up to a high level and ended up going to the Los Angeles and Barcelona Olympics with her employers. When I was twenty-four and she was just eighteen, she was based in Augsburg in Germany, less than 100km from where my wife-to-be Christine and I were living at the time, so I saw a fair amount of her then.

Later, Sue moved to Aachen and then went with her horses to shows all over Western Europe. Yet later, she worked near New York during the summer and Miami during the winter for about eight years and we saw less of each other. Nonetheless, I visited her in Florida and Connecticut a couple of times and although she was working hard during the day, we had good times in the evenings. She returned to the UK in 1999, once she could no longer work in showjumping. This is when I first realised she had a drinking problem, although I never found out if it was the physical effort required or her drinking that caused her to stop work. Like mine, her drinking was mostly in secret, and although I knew she had lost her driving license due to a DUI (driving under the influence) conviction, it was only after she died, at her wake, that I heard from her many friends and colleagues about occasions when she was drunk at work. It was very moving to hear how much they all loved her, whether she was sober or not. Personally, I rarely saw her drunk, although I did witness behaviour on one occasion that shocked me. I had gone to the cinema with her and my eldest son Matt, and she had secretly drunk in the toilets and then tried to turn the cinema seats into a bed.

I am unsure whether it was the death of our brother or the drinking culture in her industry, or maybe a combination of the two, that caused her to start her journey to alcoholism. She lived with our parents and then with me for a while. However, her drinking got too much for all of us, so she went to live in a hostel in Hull. I took her to a number of AA (Alcoholics Anonymous) meetings and supported her as best I could, but tragically she remained in denial of her addiction.

By this time (2001), I was in a position to buy a house for Sue in Hull to live in. The idea was that she could live there for free and take in two lodgers who would pay rent to cover the mortgage. I was very happy to be able to help her, but she didn't want the responsibility of finding and managing lodgers, and in hindsight, probably wanted to be able to drink alone, so she declined the offer and subsequently spent over ten years living in rented accommodation. I was a bit annoyed by her rejection to start with, but I now realise that she would have been very difficult company for the lodgers in our house. The last fourteen years of her life, before her body failed and she died aged fifty-one, were very painful for the whole family, even at a distance.

When we were children, Dad seemed to be very strict, but fair. He was a man of authority until he retired. He felt he had to be a responsible citizen, as he and his brothers looked after the dental health of about ten percent of the population of Hull, and it was in his character anyway. I once built a transmitter that could, in principle, broadcast on the police frequency, long before secure digital radio transmissions. I was very proud of my achievement and boasted of it to him, which was a mistake. Instead of being impressed, as I had hoped, he was very upset, because his reputation could have been affected by what he regarded as my criminal activities. He also didn't like me making explosives, which was easy to do at that time as even a teenager could get hold of almost any chemical ingredient they wanted. On another occasion I was the only one of a group of boys who was caught shoplifting a BB gun. This was a type of toy gun that fired plastic ball bearings. Astonishingly, this was something you could buy in any toy shop in those days. I was with a group of boys who were mostly a bit older than I was and I didn't instigate the plan, but I was the last out of the shop and so I was the one who was grabbed by the shop attendants. As I was under ten years old, the police could do nothing, but my parents were understandably horrified.

We often spent time with my father's brothers, their wives and our cousins. I was the eldest of all fifteen cousins and the most socially awkward. My favourite uncle was Uncle Roger, the youngest of the three brothers, who was more laid-back and jovial than Uncle Philip and my father Derek. Both Roger and Philip pre-deceased my father by at least a decade, both my siblings pre-deceased me and as will become clear later on, my eldest son Matt's younger siblings have pre-deceased him.

I remember Hull as a vibrant city in my teens (although at the time, I had no comparisons), offering all I needed. It didn't matter to me that it is somewhat out on a limb in the UK, at the end of both the road and railway connections. Access by ferry to the continent was easy but few people could afford to travel there. I could cycle to school or into town to access the library and cinemas and most friends were within walking or cycling distance. However, I was very glad to leave in the mid-1970s. Hull was being affected by a double decline: that of the fishing industry due to the 'Cod Wars' and second, that of the manufacturing industry due to globalisation and the Thatcher government.

I am sure I loved my parents, but I really didn't know them until I had grown up and they'd retired. We didn't express affection or emotion in our family, and we didn't talk about feelings or personal topics in general. I studied hard, not because of my parents' expectations, but because I felt I was on an academic conveyor belt. It was simply what one did.

Since my father and both his brothers had gone into dentistry, following in the footsteps of my grandfather, it might have seemed an obvious path for some of the next generation of Cowleys to take up the baton and do the same. However, my father strongly believed that the addition of fluoride to mains drinking water would significantly reduce the incidence of tooth decay and hence dentistry would become mostly cosmetic. Hence he counselled against entering dentistry and none of his or his brothers' children did. This was just as well in my case, as I had no interest in dentistry. I am so glad that I followed my passion for technology which has meant that I have enjoyed almost all of my working life.

I followed a conventional infant, primary, junior and senior school journey, all within two miles of home. I have very little recollection of my infant and primary schools and although must have learnt things, my time seemed to be mainly social, but I suspect that is the same for all. The junior and senior schools were both at Hymers College, the same school that my grandfather, father and uncles had attended. It was a pretty traditional private school, where we wore uniforms with caps all the way through until the sixth form.

There were a few times when going to school was difficult. I was bullied at school, probably because I was shy and somewhat overweight. I felt I didn't really fit in, and would rather be at home doing my hobbies, but generally I looked forward to it. I disliked team sports, especially rugby, but enjoyed squash and cricket (which I regard mostly as separate players on a field playing for the same side). I was happiest in the home environment and within the laboratories, both my own and the school ones. I had two laboratories at home, a chemistry and an electronics laboratory. As mentioned earlier, I possessed a variety of chemicals that you couldn't possibly get over the counter nowadays, but which were freely available at that time. I loved experimenting with many combinations of chemicals, including making simple explosives. In my electronics laboratory I built all manner of audio and digital devices. I was very happy in those environments with no communication with anyone else. I once did a chemistry experiment where I mixed two chemicals and put them in a small container in my pocket, for reasons that have been lost in the mists of time. What I didn't know was that if they got damp, the chemicals would spontaneously ignite. This is exactly what happened. Since my trousers were made of nylon, the pocket melted into my leg – ouch. Multiple hospital visits were required and the scar still shows. I used to take the money my mother had given me for lunch at school and spend it on electronics components, a habit which once caused me to faint at school due to hunger.

Outside school I joined the Scouts, where I enjoyed collecting badges for skills, community work and outdoor activities at camps. Within school I joined the Combined Cadet Force (CCF) – think boys playing at being soldiers – where I was not good at obeying orders. This might have been the beginnings of my rebellious streak. I remember being told to wear a pink ribbon on one wrist and blue on the other, when I consistently turned the wrong way when commanded 'Right Turn'. I left the Cadets during my O level year.

I hit teenagerhood towards the end of the sixties. The so-called Swingin' Sixties brought with them new music, new fashions and a sexual revolution in the wake of the introduction of the contraceptive pill, culminating in the Summer of Love in 1967. The headlines in Britain were dominated by Flower Power and Man landing on the Moon. Hull saw floods and a serious outbreak of polio during this decade, but people nonetheless responded to the changing times, with new nightclubs opening and a liberalisation of social attitudes. I was just a little bit too young to really notice any of this (I was still only fourteen at the end of the decade). I didn't read newspapers until I went to university and I consumed little radio or TV. Also, I was perhaps a little too engrossed in my own life.

In recent times, I have been wondering whether I took refuge in my labs. Were they my response to an environment where emotions were not talked about and there were personal dynamics I couldn't do anything about, whereas in my labs I could 'fix' things? Or was I simply naturally inclined to a concrete, practical, technical approach to the world, which led me to be emotionally uncommunicative?

I was very studious and took my schooling very seriously. It soon became clear that I was good at maths and science but not very good at other subjects. My closest friend at junior school was called David. We used to go round to each other's houses to play and to do homework. I didn't really have many friends until the sixth form. I was involved with the drama department, but mostly through helping out with the lighting and not on the stage. It was a single sex school and we mixed occasionally with a local girls' school. I was definitely interested in girls but was very shy and couldn't look a girl in the eye until I taught myself to do so when I got to university. In the sixth form, when I became a bit more sociable, I used to go out with friends to watch bands in Hull and spent a lot of time with a couple of boys who lived close by, called Bob and Nigel. They both went to Cambridge University, as I did, and Nigel was my best man in 1981 at my first wedding.

I was seventeen when I bought my first alcoholic drink. My first taste of alcohol had occurred with my parents whilst on holiday in France – they were very moderate drinkers (until my mother developed a problem after my brother died) – but it was at the Tan Hill Inn, the highest pub in England, that I bought a round for the first time. This pub is located on the Pennine Way long-distance footpath, which some schoolfriends and I were walking at the time. I remember I had two pints of bitter, and was it bitter! I didn't actually like the taste at all, but I liked the effect of the alcohol on my mood.

A few months later, I went to a party at a friend's house and took a bottle of wine, having swapped half the wine for a spirit from my parents' drinks cabinet. I don't think I shared the bottle with anyone and at the tender age of eighteen I got spectacularly drunk and had to be carried home to my parents.

The experience with my parents' drinks cabinet was an early warning shot. It should have taught me there and then that alcohol in volume is evil and that the after-effects are so severe that I should temper my drinking. But I enjoyed the sensation of mild euphoria and it didn't occur to me that this could ever become a problem.

I had been born into comfortable middle-class privilege and although I met others as a Scout and occasionally at school, my social group naturally consisted of boys of the same age, privilege and academic inclination. The boy who had a locker next to mine was extremely unhappy at school. He had been given a local authority scholarship, one of at least a hundred others, but felt isolated, particularly as he had a congenital problem. One leg was a few inches shorter than the other, which meant that he was unable to participate in sport. He studied dictionaries as a hobby. He could not share his unhappiness at home or at school, but he did confide in me. Eventually he decided he needed to be expelled, so set fire to large wastepaper bins. Although I didn't see it happen, the whole school was aware of the evacuation and arrival of several fire engines. A few days later, he told me of his expulsion, with joy in his voice, as he emptied his locker for the last time.

Overall, I didn't really enjoy school until the upper sixth form, when I got jobs in both the Chemistry and Physics laboratories and got to know the heads of those departments well. They were called Alex and Cod (at least, that was his nickname) and they took me under their wing. I would say they were my first mentors. I was very immature, but my studiousness got me into a good university.

Although it was possible to get into Oxford or Cambridge straight after A levels, it was much more usual at that time to stay on at school for a seventh term, in order to take the entrance exams and attend an interview in November, which I did. The exams were specific to Engineering Science, which I had chosen as a course at Cambridge, and for which I studied hard. Then there was something called 'Use of English', for which I hardly studied at all, and which consequently is the only formal examination or test I have ever failed. However, I had to retake and pass it, as it was needed if you wanted to go to Oxford or Cambridge. Out of the two universities, I chose Cambridge, as it was, and still is, more focused on STEM subjects than Oxford, and my school chose Fitzwilliam College for me, because a boy in the year above me had gone there to study Engineering.

After I was accepted into Cambridge, I had ten months to experience life and to grow up a little bit, or in my case, a lot, before actually leaving for university. My father had a patient who worked at our local aircraft manufacturer and through him, I got a place in the workshops, which fitted in very well with my degree choice of Engineering. However, I didn't want to spend nine months working in a factory and living at home, so in a Eureka moment in the bath, I hit upon a plan to live with my aunt in Sydney for a while. Luckily, my parents supported my plan and helped facilitate it by lending me the airfare (which in today's prices was nearly £6,000), which I managed to repay before going to university.

Flying to Australia aged eighteen was a big step, especially in 1974. Once in Sydney, there were three people who had a strong influence on my life. My aunt, Joyce, was one – she decided to use the time to teach me to think more critically about the values I had inherited from my nuclear family, in particular her sister, my mother. Our household was quite conservative and both my parents generally had right-wing views on most things. Aunt Joyce argued and discussed many things such as politics, social welfare, privilege, and education and later she told me explicitly that she had done this for my benefit, to teach me to consider and challenge what I'd been told at home. What at the time was difficult but useful was that she would change her position mid-argument to keep me on my toes intellectually. The result of this was that Aunt Joyce moved my politics from somewhat right to left of centre.

Her husband, my uncle, was a very busy gynaecologist but loved to enjoy himself. Once or twice a week we would go sailing with some of his friends on his racing yacht on Sydney Harbour. Here I was introduced to regular drinking and to laddish behaviour. No one drank to excess, as navigating a racing yacht in busy waters required a clear head, but I certainly enjoyed the buzz of some alcohol coursing through my veins.

I also worked in an electronics shop while I lived in Sydney, where my boss was Dick Smith, who went on to become an electronics tycoon and is now probably Australia's most famous entrepreneur and explorer. With hindsight, he was a major inspiration for me in becoming an entrepreneur. All in all, I was a very different person after spending six months in Australia. I had matured dramatically in many ways. It was only after this time in Sydney that I started to be able to be sociable, which made entry into the university environment much easier.

After my return from Australia in 1974 I worked in a pub in Hull until I went to Cambridge in October of that year. It was a big change for me leaving home, living with other students and a completely new structure of education, but with many opportunities for new experiences. When I arrived in Cambridge, I didn't exactly feel lonely, but I was quite apprehensive. I was very fortunate to find a like-minded individual on my corridor of six student rooms within my college. He was called Chris, and he was studying Natural Sciences, so our academic lives did not overlap, but our social lives most definitely did, and he has remained a lifelong friend.

Towards the end of my first year, I started to get involved in a social society that he'd joined, the Cambridge University Youth Hostelling Association, which was to become central to my social life then and where I developed friendships that have lasted a lifetime. The first week or two was a blur of learning about the college, learning about what social groups I could join, learning new regimes, and working out how to timetable my own life. Doing Engineering Science meant I had a greater academic workload compared to, for instance, the English students like my friend from Hull days, Nigel, who claimed to only go to one or two lectures per term (he later acted as my best man). I had many lectures and practicals during term time, including Saturday mornings. I had programmed the Hull University computer whilst at school in the early 1970s, so I soon got involved with programming the university IBM mainframe, meeting other like-minded programmers late at night. We commonly did this on a Friday because we had much faster access to the computer outside academic office hours.

I went to Cambridge University with few expectations except that I wanted to enjoy myself and work out what I wanted to do with the next stage of my life. Many students find when they go to university that they may have been doing very well at school, but that at university, there are many people who are brighter and more capable than they are, and I was no different. I had to work much harder than I expected to maintain reasonable results in the various assignments that we were set. This meant hours in the library and in my room studying. Of course this was before personal computers, so everything was done with pen and paper – luckily the slide rules and log tables I had been using at school were now obsolete. Fitting everything in was really difficult, especially in the second year, and so the thing that I had to let go of was sleep, probably existing on less than six hours per night during the week.

The terms are very short at Cambridge – just eight weeks long with a shorter summer term, when exams are held. It is said that you have to work harder at Cambridge because your academic time is a smaller proportion of the calendar year. For me, however, the terms were too short to fit everything in, which meant I had to spend four weeks after the official end of the academic year in a so-called summer vacation term, as well as use the Easter holiday for the practical work that was required for the course, which I organised in Hull at Remploy (an employment service for disabled people). The first two weeks involved learning how to weld, at which I was spectacularly bad compared to others. The second two weeks were much more enjoyable and fitted in with my skills as I learnt and practised repairing televisions. In those days, televisions used valves, long before transistors and flat screens.

The second year sped by with academic work and running a travelling discotheque called Brainchild. My friend Chris and I bought this disco from two veterinary postgraduates. The two vets had run it for a while but felt the time had come where they ought to concentrate on their studies and they kindly lent us the money (£20 each) which we paid back from profits. One of them had a minivan that was just big enough to carry the equipment and vinyls and hence provided the transport to and from gigs, taking one-third of the profits. This was a tiny business, more of a hobby really, but it taught Chris and me about marketing, selling, pricing, customer relationships, providing a service, sourcing vinyl singles, accounting, and repairing the equipment. Many years later, I worked out that we earned less than what would have been the minimum wage in those days, but it sure was fun. In all cases, we had access to drink and any food provided and we loved entertaining and making people happy on the dancefloor.

A few events stand out. One was in the Cambridge Guildhall, where we were the accompaniment to a band who wouldn't let us use their amplification equipment. This was fine before they came on, but when they went off for a break after playing for a while, our speakers were so under-powered that no one could hear our music because their hearing had been affected by the band. At one disco, Chris and I decided to test our bladder volumes – he won after consuming over a gallon of beer before needing the loo. The only event we did in someone's home resulted in the neighbours calling the police and making us stop.

I struggled with choosing a specialist subject within Engineering for my final year. Engineering Science at Cambridge at that time appeared to be mostly applied mathematics, whereas I love being practical. I enjoy getting engaged in solving real world problems using practical techniques. So I chose the single year Computer Science Tripos (Cambridge and Oxford call this a Tripos after a three-legged stool), which had only just become an undergraduate option. It was an easy choice to make as I had been programming the university mainframe since I came up to

Cambridge. It did mean yet another long vacation term: four weeks in Cambridge after the end of the normal academic year, working very hard, with many fewer students about.

Computer Science wasn't what I expected. Although there was plenty of programming, there was also a lot of theory, which turned out to be of little benefit once I'd moved into the workplace. Still, I enjoyed it a lot more than the final year options of Engineering.

That year also sped by. By this time, Chris and I had sold the travelling discotheque, freeing up some time, but I'd met a girl at ballroom dancing, a first-year medical student at Girton College called Sue. I was a member of four committees and part of the youth hostelling group, and now I also spent a lot of time with Sue.

I'd started Cambridge with a scholarship called an Exhibition, which gave £40 a year (the equivalent of £500 in 2023) as a grant. The first year I spent that on a calculator from Hewlett-Packard and the second year on books. Achieving this scholarship in the second and third years also gave me the opportunity to live within the college if I wanted. In those days, the alternative for most students at my college was living with a landlady in a house nearby, which had a huge disadvantage in terms of disturbing the household when one came in late, possibly with friends. So my room in college became a focus for friends to come back to late in the evening and then dissipate back to their various rooms in the neighbourhood, creeping in quietly. This helped gradually turn me into a more confident and sociable person.

I did have a lot of fun, maybe too much, and got caught for a couple of pranks while there. One was to file down my room key with the help of a much more geeky friend than me, so it became a master key. This allowed access into anyone's room. We only actually used this twice: once on the president of what in Cambridge is called the Junior Common Room, an elected student representative body, to leave a beer barrel in his room. He was quite confused about this but took it in good spirits and played a very effective prank back, by impersonating, in writing, the tutor in charge of disciplining students. He typed a well-worded letter on college letterhead threatening all kinds of punishments and added a forged signature at the bottom. For weeks, I walked in fear of these disciplinary measures, until he owned up. The college was less impressed when we did something (I can't now even remember what it was) within the cleaners' cupboard, when I was genuinely threatened with being expelled, which was only avoided by me grovelling to a senior member of the college. On another occasion, scaffolding was being used for maintenance and with a friend I climbed on to the flat roof and tied paper tape from one end of the college to the other. The paper tape came from the computer laboratory and I had programmed a spectacularly silly bit of text on it which read: *Roses are red, violets are blue, some poems rhyme, but this one doesn't.*

I am not sure how and why I developed anti-establishment tendencies – I don't remember feeling a need to stand out from the others, nor a feeling of inferiority. I clearly didn't understand the boundaries between a prank and a college rule. Of course, this is what entrepreneurs do: challenge existing practices with a drive to disrupt something, so maybe for me this was an early sign of the risk-taking entrepreneur and angel investor I was going to become.

I was nineteen when I went to Cambridge and twenty-two when I left, ready for the working world as an adult. My levels of drinking, which had started back in Australia, had also gone up and I was definitely regarded as one of the heavier drinkers by my friends in Cambridge. A group of engineers from one of the other colleges and I used to go out a few times a term to drink. The heaviest drinker of the group didn't like beer, so he used to drink vodka and tomato juice. Unless he has stopped drinking since, I would be surprised if he is still alive. My drinking did lead to some incidents which seemed amusing at the time, such as falling off my bike, but I never blacked out and never forgot what I'd done the night before. It was during my university time that I had my worst hangover ever. Some of us were travelling via Interrail and one night we slept in an olive grove in Corfu after three of the four of us drank a bottle of ouzo each (after beer and wine) in a beach restaurant. Nearly fifty years later, I still can't stand the smell of aniseed. But this was the start of my journey to alcoholism.

I had been a very shy boy at a single sex school but that didn't mean that I was not interested in girls. I was nineteen years old when I first kissed a girl, facilitated for both of us by alcohol at a friend's party in his room at my college. We tried to build a relationship over the following weeks, but it all fizzled out, I suspect because of my immaturity.

On New Year's Eve 1974, after my first term at Cambridge, I was invited by a friend to a party on a farm near Hull and there met a girl called Deborah whose party it was. We started a relationship which lasted on and off for nearly four years. She came from a family farm and was studying Agriculture at Newcastle University. I used to hitchhike from Cambridge to Newcastle about once a term to be with her and of course we'd see each other a lot during the vacation. We would holiday together and we both got to know each other's families very well. We had great times together, and although there was the possibility of taking over the large arable family farm with her, I saw my life in technology in London. We separated a couple of times and then got back together again, before finally splitting up in autumn of 1978 rather dramatically on a crowded train from London to Hull, within earshot of dozens of passengers.

Most vacations I also went away, commonly hiking in Snowdonia (Eryri) or the Lake District with the youth hostelling group. The other long-term friends from Cambridge came from my Computer Science course, but none from Engineering. I also met many people at Fitzwilliam College, but none have remained friends, unless they were part of the youth hostelling society.

I realised that I was likely to end up in situations where I had to be part of a group of people running an organisation and thus I set myself the task of experiencing that by joining the committees of four groups in Cambridge. These comprised of the university Youth Hostelling Association, the Engineering Society (which mostly organised site visits, such as visiting Heathrow to board a stationary Concorde), the Photographic Society (think processing monochrome photos in the dark) and what was then the Tape Recording Society. The last of those allowed me to meet some very interesting people in the Hi-Fi world, including Ray Dolby of noise-reduction fame.

In the three years that I was at university I also worked in the vacations. For two years running I worked in the Lord Nelson, a pub in Hull on what was regarded as one of the poorest estates in Britain. The landlord, Brian, was lovely and a great employer. The clientele were mainly older people – those over forty, up into their eighties. I worked with two close friends who were also at Cambridge University, and we must have seemed a strange trio to them, although we lived only five minutes away by bicycle. I learnt a lot about human nature working in that pub. Very generously, and as was normal in those days, the standard tip was half a pint, although of course not everyone tipped. One New Year's Eve there were lots of tips: too many to drink during opening hours. So after closing time, Brian had a lock-in with just staff and family and we worked our way through all our 'tips'. The others drank sensibly, but I couldn't. I wasn't able to stop drinking once I had started. It got so out of control that I ended up snogging Brian's mother and falling into a hedge on the way home.

In the summers I also worked at the Bird's Eye factory in west Hull. The first two summers I was on the fish finger line, where my only role for an entire eight-hour shift was to pick up a heavy tray of frozen fish finger material, rotate it 180 degrees and knock it on a flat surface so that the frozen slab came away from the metal tray. This was a production line, so I had to keep up with the freezer and the conveyor belt. One time I was rushed to the sick bay, when I dropped the heavy metal tray onto a finger. The nurse stabbed a red-hot needle into my fingernail to release the pressure of the blood blister. I fainted, although the relief was extreme.

We had breaks, of course, and I spent those talking to my co-workers. Many of them, especially the men, had been to borstal and/or prison. Every fourth or fifth word was a swear word, and I must have seemed quite alien to them, so I kept quiet and listened. Many years later I would spend time with people with similar life experiences in Alcoholics Anonymous meetings and I am sure the factory floor interactions were useful for me at AA. I passed the time at the conveyor belt dreaming about buying an expensive camera and what I would do with that.

In my third summer, after I graduated, I worked on the frozen pea line, on what was a very cushy job. Two of us directed incoming pea trailers to the appropriate hoppers. It was rare that we both needed to work simultaneously so I read a novel on each shift. The shifts were twelve hours long and we swapped between the day shift and the night shift and back again on Sundays. Every other Sunday we worked sixteen hours. The pay was tremendous, equating to around £1,000 a week in 2023. But the best part of working there was getting to know Tony. He had also been at my school, but the year below, so I didn't know him before we worked on the line together. He was doing a Chemistry degree at Manchester and was about to train to be an accountant. We became extremely close friends and spent much time together once he had moved to London. He died tragically early at forty-one of leukaemia, a father of two.

In the final year at Cambridge, we were confronted with what is called the 'milk round', where companies come to universities to recruit students. I didn't come out of university desperate to make societal change. I wasn't interested in politics, nor in the City of London where serious money could be made, but more in enjoying my working life. I decided that I wanted to remain in computer programming and was interviewed by ten companies, from which I got nine job offers. It was not an easy choice and I chose Logica because they offered more projects using a new technology called the microprocessor.

I had done very well in Engineering, achieving a 2.1 in years one and two, but the exam format in Computer Science didn't suit me, as there was much less mathematics and formulae and more writing. Despite extensive revision, I sat one exam at the end of the year where I could not answer a single question and left as soon as I could. This meant I only managed a 2.2 in the final year, but it actually made no difference to any of the job offers. However, my father was quite angry about this. I'm not sure whether this was because of the mediocre result itself or the fact that I'd told my grandmother about it before I told him.

In any event, there I was, a slightly immature but brainy young man, straight out of university, about to start a conventional job, with the confidence of a comfortable middle-class upbringing and no idea of the horrors that life had in store for him.

Chapter 3

First Encounter with Death

The last few days of university were bittersweet. I was glad to be entering the world of work and leaving academia, but sad to be leaving Cambridge and my friends and fellow students with whom I'd shared learning and adventures. As it turned out, a core of about a dozen of us are still spending time together even now, nearly fifty years later. For me, as for so many people, the friends I made at university remained so all through my life.

I have three distinct memories from my last week at university. Firstly, my girlfriend Sue and I agreed that we would separate. We'd been together since the beginning of my third year, but she was going to be in Cambridge for a further five years as a medical student, and also her father did not like me. I suspected that as he was a widower and Sue was an only child, he was, not unnaturally, protective of her and to make things worse, I had let my hair grow down to my shoulders. The breakup was a sad but sensible decision. Secondly, I remember that one fellow Fitzwilliam College student wished me 'a good life'. This phrase struck me so powerfully at the time that I have adopted it and continued to use it myself over the years if I expect never to meet someone again. Thirdly, I was part of a final prank. A group of us had gone to a friend's room in another college and turned his room upside down. This person discovered who was responsible and for some reason, his retaliation was inflicted on me. Overnight, he moved my fridge from the student common room on my corridor to the college gardens and placed two explosive crow-scarers inside, which were a bit like sticks of dynamite. He lit them and closed the door. So, instead of passing the fridge on to another student, I had to get it to the recycling centre (the dump in those days)!

The summer was spent working in the pea department at Bird's Eye back home in Hull, on a short holiday with my parents and preparing to move to London. One of my university friends by the name of Mark had also joined Logica, and had taken a room in a shared house in Shepherd's Bush which belonged to the parents of yet another computer scientist friend. However, Mark had immediately been sent to Logica's office in New York (lucky him!) so I took his room.

This was an easy landing in terms of finding accommodation. Meanwhile, my parents had bought me a car similar to my mother's: a tiny Honda with literally a motorcycle engine and a top speed of 65mph, so I packed up all my possessions and drove down from Hull to London. That was me officially leaving home, never to return to live. I had 'fled the nest'. I felt very happy to leave the (by then) decaying city of Hull behind me. I am still proud of being from Yorkshire, less so from Hull. All the same, I was somewhat daunted by the idea of building a new life in the 'big smoke'.

Settling into an office job was not difficult, as the work was enjoyably challenging. Most of my Computer Science studies at Cambridge were of little relevance outside academia, but my hundreds of nights programming definitely stood me in good stead. The people were interesting; most were under thirty and great fun to be with. I was newly single so joined the company's darts team and weekends were spent with new and old friends. Many of my student friends had moved into jobs in London and were to remain in or near London for the rest of their lives.

In the first few months I worked on several small projects, learning about aspects of being in business: sales, marketing, costing, project planning, delivering, and new hardware and software. I was really in my element, becoming a more rounded commercial person and not just a computer programmer.

Within six weeks, the whole company was flown to Jersey for a weekend of strategy and enjoyment. Shortly after that I was relocated to Bath to write software to monitor and control electricity sub-stations throughout the country for a large industrial company in Chippenham. This was not what I expected, as although the work was interesting, I had little contact with head office, which was probably detrimental to my career at Logica. I made the most of life in Bath for nearly a year, getting into activities such as bell ringing, car maintenance and of course socialising. Deborah, my ex-girlfriend with the farming background who'd been at Newcastle University, had decided to do a teacher training course in Bath, and we resurrected our relationship for what would turn out to be one year.

I enjoyed the work, although it was not very taxing. In those days we would create software in pencil on paper, someone would type it up, and then we would run it on a hardware simulator with the results coming back the next day, a process unimaginably different from modern software techniques. The project came to a close the following summer and I was relocated back to London. Part of my training involved a flight to Sunderland in north-east England to sell a system for a crane manufacturer to monitor the weight being lifted and hence prevent cranes accidentally tipping over. We lost the proposal, but I learnt a lot from the trip. It was the first time I had done any selling, in the sense of going out and trying to persuade someone. I was young, probably quite cocky, going up north with my posh accent, and I hadn't been trained in how to relate to a potential buyer.

Once back in London, I was put on a project for the Post Office to automate an alarm system in the main international telephone exchange by the Thames. This was very interesting, especially as I was involved in client meetings. The project was handed over but never used. This was during a period when trade unions were very strong and using the system would have led to many redundancies, which they naturally resisted.

I then joined a project to automate a brewery site in south Wales for Whitbread. We were a team of about a dozen staff from Logica and we needed to be on site in order to test the system which was designed to brew beer from malt, hops, yeast and water into the finished product. I was on the project for about eighteen months and we lived in south Wales in a couple of rented houses. There were about ten of us on the project, so we rented two houses near the brewery. None of us was over the age of thirty. We really threw ourselves into the project, working from 9am to 6pm, eating, and then often going back to work until midnight. It was on this project that I introduced a software bug that took six weeks to fix, as it was very intermittent, and after the software met the bug, the system behaviour depended on the temperature reading in one of the fermenting vessels, which varied hour by hour.

Those with partners went home at weekends and I commonly stayed to go hiking in the Brecon Beacons with a friend or my girlfriend. At this time I had been going out with an artist by the name of Cathy who lived in Bath and who opened my eyes to many things such as the beauty of nature. There were still many aspects of life I had yet to discover aged twenty-three!

I was introduced to skiing by a friend, David, from Logica and had a great week in Italy with a group of Logica colleagues: lots of falls, lots of drinking. The day I got home I went to a party with David, and there I met my future wife, Christine. Christine had known David for several years through mountain climbing and when she moved to London, they formed a casual relationship. We had both arrived a little early and started chatting. We hit it off really well straightaway, although I was a little in awe of her accomplishments. She was three years older than me, a competent skier and rock climber, and she had been in the workplace as an environmental consultant for a few years. We chatted and danced all evening, and as we walked back to our own cars, we swapped telephone numbers (landline numbers of course, this was a different era!) and agreed to meet a few days later to see the Alan Ayckbourn play *Bedroom Farce*. We had many things in common: love of the outdoors, travel and socialising, and we were intellectually similar. It didn't take long for a friendship to become intense love. Both of us really enjoyed our work and were very keen to continue that but without a particular career path in mind. We wanted a good work/life balance, so soon started plotting a journey through life together.

Christine had studied Geography at Cambridge and worked in Edinburgh. She'd relocated to London after her fiancé was killed in a rock-climbing accident to join what was probably the first environmental consultancy in the UK. We generally spent weekends at her flat in London or hiking in south Wales. After a while, we decided to buy a house together, so Christine sold her Edinburgh flat and we bought a terraced house in north Islington.

When we stayed with my parents, Christine slept in my old room, and I had to sleep in the family caravan on the drive, so you can imagine how upset they were when we told them we were buying a house together without being married. They came to visit me in London and I was taken out to the Ritz Hotel for lunch so that they could tell me exactly what they thought about it. It seemed out of character for my parents, but whatever they said and however they said it, it was not going to change my mind. Perhaps their strong reaction was related to the fact that as a family we were still grieving from my brother's death earlier that year.

Christine and I were living in London when we found out about David's illness in early 1979. I don't exactly remember how and when I was told, and in fact I don't know whether I understood straightaway that leukaemia was a type of cancer. With no internet, I knew little about cancer and don't remember asking anyone. When I had left for London, David was still living with our parents and working in the Humbrol factory. He wasn't sure what he wanted to do with his life, so his girlfriend Susie's parents said they'd pay for Susie and David, who had been together for about a year and half by then, to have a holiday with them in New Zealand.

The day before their departure, we took them to Heathrow to stay overnight and to see them off with the whole family the next day. It was December and I was sharing a room with David in the hotel near Heathrow, as our parents wouldn't let Susie and him share a room. I remember David showing me the engagement ring he was taking over to propose to Susie on Christmas Eve, after they got there. They stayed in New Zealand for over a year, working and living in Auckland, which David really enjoyed. All went well, until Susie noticed that David started to have breathing difficulties and would even have brief fainting spells. Susie and her parents urged him to see a doctor, which David was reluctant to do, saying he was just a bit tired. At first, it did not occur to them that there might be something seriously wrong, so the diagnosis, when it came, was a massive shock to them all. David called our parents and then faced the decision whether to return to the UK for treatment or stay in New Zealand. They decided to return to the UK immediately and I was so keen to meet them at the airport that I got a traffic fine for driving on the hard shoulder on the motorway to Heathrow.

Treatment was started immediately, and both David and Susie found jobs locally in Hull: David as a refrigeration engineer and Susie with a finance company. He told no one at work of his illness, as he didn't want anyone to treat him any differently because of it. Cancer treatment has advanced hugely over the years, of course, but this was 1979, and the outlook was not good. I was told only very recently by Susie, i.e. forty-three years later, that she and David didn't in fact know this. The information flow went from the doctors through our father, and he controlled and filtered what he passed on to David and Susie, keeping a great deal from them, particularly if it was bad news. He would have done this with the best of intentions, of course, but it is unimaginable to think of this happening nowadays. Susie and David simply lived with the grind of having the treatment and then David feeling very ill for days afterwards. His treatments would be scheduled on a Friday, so he could get over the worst after-effects at the weekend.

Despite the challenges, three months after they returned to the UK, David and Susie got married and moved into a flat together. I was best man at the wedding, and although David had Bell's palsy from the chemotherapy, and one side of his mouth was hanging down, it was a joyous event. I was almost as nervous giving my best man's speech on that day as I was at my own wedding two years later. The bride and bridegroom looked stunning and his cancer was completely forgotten for the day.

I was living in London with Christine at the time and came back to see them once a month, in their flat in Hull. David remained stable for some time. However, after five months, it was decided to cease chemo and let the illness take its course. I didn't understand the reasoning at the time, but I do now. The treatment was stopped because it was no longer working, and his quality of life was badly affected. He was having physical problems and in fact, just before Christmas he had a car accident. He was told to stop driving, which was a huge blow for him because he loved cars. His mental and physical acuity deteriorated even further from that moment onwards. Even then, Susie had no idea that David's life was close to the end. No one had given them a prognosis, told them what was going to happen or how long David would probably have left.

When Susie was told by their GP, as she let him out of the flat after a home visit, that "it was a matter of days," she first of all didn't understand what he meant, before collapsing on the floor with the shock of realisation. She made some excuse to David about going out and went and sat on a chair in their local chemist crying desperately, with the people around her in true British fashion just leaving her to get on with it. She then had to go back and tell David the news. They cried together and he made her promise that she wouldn't 'do anything silly', that is, take her own life. Susie puts their ignorance down in part to our father and the medics keeping things from them, but also to them being young and a bit naïve, never having heard of young people dying of things like cancer, and of course the fact that it was more difficult to find things out before the age of the internet.

When I was told that David probably didn't have very long to live, I was in Yorkshire on a business trip with my boss, Greg, and he let me keep the hire car so I could drive to Hull to see my brother. I met my parents at David and Susie's flat. After greeting me, my mother asked if I wanted to see David to say goodbye. I clearly remember feeling quite anxious about going into the room, as this was my first personal experience of being with a loved one at the end of their life. Having gathered my courage, I went into the room to see him for the last time. He was sitting in a chair and the curtains were closed. It was January, so it got dark quite early. He couldn't speak any longer but his eyes were still open and I felt he still recognised me. There was no one else in the room, no medical team at all, since it was now just a waiting game. In the end I was not particularly upset at that moment, and I didn't cry. I think some of the grieving had already happened because I'd visited him regularly since May and seen him gradually decline. I recognised that he was on a pathway to death.

That afternoon, on the 18th of January 1980, Christine caught the train up from London. I picked her up from the station and in the early evening, we visited David and Susie together and then made our way to the house of my favourite uncle Roger and his wife. It was while we were there that my father rang to say David had died. I hugged my uncle and aunt and we immediately drove the fifteen minutes back. Once more I went into the room, this time to see his body. It was the first time I had seen a dead body, but I still didn't cry. I spent some time alone with him, saying goodbye and apologising for what I thought was his solitude at the point of dying. I had not realised that Susie had been with him when he died.

The funeral was a few days later at the local crematorium, where finally I did cry. David's death was not really mentioned after that. No one spoke about anything. In those days, it was normal for people generally to put a brave face on things, show stoicism and keep a stiff upper lip, and it was definitely like that in our family. Susie remembers that David, towards the end, was quite obsessed with the fact that his parents had never held him and said we love you and we don't want you to die. He knew they loved him, but it wasn't said. Sadly, it was probably David's death that drove my mother to alcoholism.

Christine and I went back to London and carried on with our life together. Later that very same week, we marked the first anniversary of our meeting, and three months later we were on our way to live in Germany, a move that I am convinced was related to David's death. In the months leading up to it, I was working on the Whitbread brewery project in Wales, leading a small team. I got on well with the German supplier of some of the hardware for the project, Lothar Ulbrich, and he had made it clear to me that he would quite like to have me working for him. I had talked this through a bit with Christine, who was supportive, but I hadn't made any move toward actually doing anything about it. My brother's death gave me the impetus to grasp this opportunity. My outlook had changed. I felt life was too short to just work up the career ladder at Logica. This opportunity meant I could work for a small company and we could live in a place that was more pleasant and interesting to us, because of the hiking and skiing and so on. It felt like a really big risk, to relocate to a country where I couldn't speak the language, to leave behind friends, to simply move there together with Christine. Losing my brother pushed me over the edge to take that risk. It was not about running away, just about taking an opportunity. That opportunity was strong, but I needed a trigger to leave the comfortable place where I was, to move on, and that trigger was provided by what happened to David. The move also meant that I was very busy indeed, organising everything by phone, telex and letter. I didn't have time to dwell on any feelings or thoughts, and this is a coping mechanism that I have turned to over and over again in my life.

Many years later, with hindsight, knowledge and professional help, I began to realise that addressing a problem and processing it is a much more healthy way of living one's life than burying it under busy-ness. Of course, at the time of David's death, the idea of therapy was not widespread, and on top of that, as I've said already, we were not a family that shared emotions. So Christine and I went off to Germany, where our new life took our minds off our grief for David, his life cut so short, denying him and me a future as brothers in adult life.

Chapter 4
Fatherhood and Business Success

The move to Germany was immense and a significant challenge. My German was pretty basic (I had studied it for O level, the equivalent of a modern GCSE), but Christine had spent her gap year in Vienna and was pretty fluent. German bureaucracy lived up to the national stereotype, so that opening a bank account, getting a resident's permit and work permit and many other necessary procedures were far from straightforward. We wanted to import our car, but it failed its import TÜV (a road safety certification) at the first attempt, despite it being a left-hand-drive Volkswagen Golf that had been exported from Germany a few weeks before. It was also quite a job furnishing our flat since it was common then for everything – up to and including light fittings – to be removed by the previous tenants. Nonetheless, these problems were all solved, and I settled into my new job and way of life. I loved my work. I had much more independence than in the 600-strong company in London and fascinating access to the trials and tribulations of building an early-stage company.

We built up a new social life and made new friends. As is common with expats, we met quite a few couples where one partner was English and the other German, with English as our common language. In those days, in southern Germany, English was very rarely spoken by anyone over thirty. We lived next door to a Bavarian and even after we had been living there for four years and I could speak good German, I still only understood perhaps one word in ten of his dialect.

With hindsight, the small company that I joined, Ulbrich Automation, which had supplied Whitbread, was suffering from what is sometimes referred to as 'creeping excellence'. This means that the product was in a permanent state of development and Ulbrich was always short of money. I was privy to some of this, because the founder, Lothar Ulbrich, and I became drinking buddies. He also owned a local music bar (called Nota Bene), and we used to go out to lunch once or twice a week. I was responsible for writing the software for the existing and new products and also helped out at trade shows throughout Germany.

Eventually the cash shortage proved too much for Lothar and he sold the company to one of its customers, Heckler and Koch, who make weapons. A colleague and I decided we didn't want to work there and would form a new company, called Gercom, with completely new products, but initially selling to similar customers. My last contact with Lothar was twenty years later in Munich, when I arranged to meet him for a catch-up and learnt a very valuable lesson, unbeknownst to him – namely that it's really important to avoid regret. I found him to be difficult company as he felt he had not been treated fairly in life. On the one hand, I was somewhat sorry for him, but on the other hand I took away with me an increased sense that regret is not constructive. I was very sorry that Lothar hadn't been able to move on, and it was quite painful to see him. Lothar had been a friend and one of my mentors and that made it feel even worse.

At Gercom, I was responsible for hardware and software design and setting up distributors outside Germany. As with any startup, this was a full-on job, and I was often working long hours into the early evenings but never from home or on vacation, as this was before the Windows-based personal computer and the internet, so we could only work from the office. There was a very clear delineation between home and work in those days.

Christine settled into her role as the German agent for the UK environmental consultancy that she had been working for in London. One of her first jobs was to translate German environmental law into English for the UK government. Many years later she helped define environmental law for the Baltic States as part of their entry to the EU. All her work was done by hand, writing on paper, and communication was by telephone and occasional telex.

We built friendships with locals and expats, spent many weekends skiing or hiking in the nearby mountains, enjoyed having Munich almost on our doorstep, had a very active social life, and travelled extensively within the Alps, as well as back to the UK to see family and friends and further afield. We got married in 1981 in the UK, and our honeymoon was in California and Nevada. We both loved travel — we hiked for seventeen days around Annapurna in Nepal in 1983 and spent a few days in India, where we caught a train from Agra (having seen the Taj Mahal) to Delhi that was running a mere thirty hours late.

When I was growing up, my father was very keen on older cars and in the late fifties he used to rally, but during my period in Germany, I developed a passion for newer cars and I have been fortunate enough to have owned a string of German performance cars ever since.

Shortly after we married, Christine moved to Hong Kong for about six months to undertake an environmental impact assessment for the new airport (which in the end was delayed by a decade for political and economic reasons). This meant that I lived by myself and spoke much less English daily, so that when Christine returned, my German was better than hers. I had even got to point of dreaming in German.

A year after we had got married, we decided to try for children. Our first child, Matt, was conceived soon after we returned from Nepal.

This, of course, led to huge excitement and more life planning. When we moved to Germany, we'd intended to stay for two years. We'd already almost doubled that time, and we knew that having a baby was going to lead to a radical change in our lifestyle, so we started to plan to return to the UK – partly to be nearer family, partly as I wanted to found my own business and didn't believe my written German would ever be good enough to do this in Germany, and partly because we were fed up with renting and wanted to live in our own house again.

Matt was born a couple of weeks late, in January 1984. Two weeks earlier, we had been to a very loud Meatloaf concert, where it was obvious from Matt's vigorous kicking that he was aware of the music, so we retreated to the back of the hall. The day before Matt was born, I drove Christine into the maternity hospital. That morning, I checked with the hospital that Christine was comfortable and then went out to lunch, pre mobile phones of course! However, things started to move quite quickly with Christine's labour, so I had to be tracked down at a local pub where my colleague and I had gone for our lunch break without thinking that I might need to be contacted. I rushed to her bedside with less than an hour to spare. Both mother and baby were healthy, and Christine was given stout to help with milk production. The rules meant she had to stay in hospital for several days, which was tough for her as her room overlooked Lake Starnberg to the snowy German Alps.

In fact, we took Matt skiing a mere four weeks later, taking turns to ski or to hold him, despite the disapproving looks and comments from elderly Austrian skiers about it being too cold for a small baby. Subsequently, Matt has spent at least seven years of his life as a ski instructor, so starting him early on the slopes can't have done him any harm!

I regard my four-and-a-half years in southern Germany as a very important part of my life — I had taken the plunge to become an entrepreneur, and Christine and I had a very strong relationship, although with much hindsight, we didn't communicate well about emotional issues. Neither of us had grown up in families where emotions were discussed and we hadn't learnt to be aware of, let alone express, our feelings. We also both drank too much. It didn't help that in Bavaria at that time a half-litre of beer was cheaper than a soft drink. Nonetheless, we had a fabulous pre-kids time travelling throughout Europe and some of the world. I had been intellectually challenged by learning a new language and by building a company. I was slimmer and fitter than at any other time in my life. I was able to satisfy my technical curiosity and drive cars fast; there were few autobahn speed limits in Germany in the 1980s, so 130mph was a typical cruising speed for me. We made new friends and both our sets of parents visited us regularly, as did other UK friends, and we often saw my sister as she spent most of those five years living in Germany, working as a groom.

Christine and I had bought a house in Islington near Finsbury Park in 1979 and on moving to Germany, we rented that out, initially to friends and later to tenants we had never met. We decided to do that without an agent, which led to some annoying issues such as the tenants calling a plumber on a Sunday to fix a leaking washer at a cost of £350 in today's money, and the discovery of very large wet rot fungi when we took the house back. In the meantime, a university friend of Christine and his wife were selling their cottage in the northern Lake District in the UK and we bought it from them to use as a holiday base, which it was for many years.

Camdata Limited was founded in late 1983 to prepare for our return to the UK. When we set it up, it wasn't clear what we were going to do. I just knew I wanted to have my own company once we got back to the UK and not return to employment. In the meantime, I acted as the UK import agent for Gercom and Christine used her contacts to set up as a self-employed environmental consultant. We moved back to the UK when

Matt was eight months old, after a fortnight's holiday on the east coast of Canada, the USA and seeing friends in the Bahamas.

Life was good and we were looking forward to our new life in the UK, as were our families. It was my dream to build up the company, then sell it and retire before my 40th birthday.

Once back in London, I subcontracted as a software engineer for an ex-colleague from Logica days while I developed Camdata into the UK distributor for Gercom. Christine immediately started finding clients and so we employed a live-in au pair, whom we had met through our two closest friends in Germany, called David and Ros. We used to spend many weekends with the four of us and David had replaced me as a software engineer at Ulbrich, later joining me at Gercom.

The au pair's name was Nicky. She was a young Austrian and lived with us for a year before returning to Innsbruck. She was succeeded by an au pair from Luxembourg and two Polish au pairs before we had a full-time nanny.

The first thing to do was to move out of London. Although we had a three-bedroom house, we didn't want to bring up children in inner London, and decided we would move to somewhere with an established electronics industry to support the intended growth of Camdata, not too far from London. This meant going west or north.

Christine was an only child. Her father, Bill, was Head of Physics at Taunton School, a truly lovely man, and a good and caring teacher. Her mother, Mary, was quite different, and although we both loved her father, we both struggled with Mary who, for example, would regularly kick her husband under the table (the winces were visible), if she wanted him to stop speaking. They had rented a house from Taunton School and then bought a house with a large garden nearby when he retired. Christine was sent to boarding school in Salisbury, spending the winters with friends in Obergurgl, an Austrian ski resort, and the summers with a school friend on the Mediterranean. Relations were so strained that one time, years later, when Bill and Mary came to stay with me and our three boys, Christine went to stay in a local hotel in order to avoid them.

When it came to choosing where to move, it was therefore obvious that we were not going to go west out of London, in the direction of Taunton, but to Cambridge, where we had both been students.

We'd bought the cottage in the Lake District directly from our friends, and so we decided to sell our house in London also without using an estate agent. I produced some home printed particulars with a glued-on colour photo and advertised in *The Observer* newspaper. It must have been a good time to sell, as we sold within a couple of weeks. Negotiating the price was fun. Buyers pay stamp duty tax, which at that time started at £30,001, but we wanted to sell the house for £31,000 (worth £120,000 in 2023). So we thought of a cunning plan: we sold the house for £30,000 and the decrepit garden shed for £1,000 (£3,800 at 2023 prices!).

But where to buy a house? We had developed a close friendship with an ex-colleague from Logica called Alan Dunckley and his wife Sue, who had moved to a place near Ely, north of Cambridge, and so we stayed with them while we searched for somewhere to live.

We ended up buying the former post office in a village called Earith, about five miles from them. This house had a fun feature: the Royal Mail post box, still in use, was set in its front wall, and somehow we had the key to the inside, which led to a few practical tricks such as pulling a letter into the box, much to the surprise of the person posting it. I'm sure it was totally against the Royal Mail rules for us to have access to a public letterbox!

It was big enough for up to three children, an au pair, an office for Christine and an office/workshop for me, plus a large narrow garden. It was thirty minutes' drive from Cambridge, with easy access to walks and the River Ouse, on which we had a home-built wooden dinghy, within the Fens.

The next three years were busy times, building up our businesses and having two more boys, Ian and Alan, with less than four years between the eldest and youngest. Christine decided she wanted three children in case one of them died, a very unusual way of thinking, but I was happy with her suggestion. This was six years after my brother had died and it was still a painful memory.

I employed two people as Camdata grew: initially Alan Dunkley's wife Sue, then another Sue, and Mike, whose twin brother Pete was still working for me twenty-five years later. Things were going very well, so we looked at moving the company out of the family home. We came across a Victorian school in a nearby village that had been converted for commercial use many years before. It was, unsurprisingly, called the Old School, and had been owned by a couple of businesses since then, both of which had gone bust. We sold the cottage in the Lake District and lent the proceeds to Camdata to buy the building. This was before Cambridge prices started to affect areas further out in the Fens, and we paid just £28,000 (£95,000 in 2023 prices) for a 3,000-square-foot building.

Camdata had started designing and manufacturing its own computer hardware products, so at the same time as buying the Old School, I took on a Production Director, called Phil, and the company began to take off. We had customers, products, processes, intellectual property and enough profit to employ a sales team, more engineers and support staff. We had customers in many sectors, such as manufacturing, telecommunications, finance, oil and gas, food production, defence. This meant we were not dependent on any one customer or any one sector. By late 1989, the business had grown to employ twenty-six people, with no external equity finance but simply bank borrowing.

Once the Old School was established and Camdata had moved out of our home, we started looking for a larger house near a suitable school for the boys.

It would have made sense to move nearer to or even into Cambridge, but we couldn't afford what we wanted, and so finally it came down to a choice between two houses, both near good schools and both, coincidentally, also near Air Force bases. It was difficult to decide how much of a noise nuisance each airfield might be, so to find this out, Christine worked from her car for one day in the vicinity of each airbase in turn, listening to aircraft movements. This would have been so much easier with the internet. As it turned out, on that particular day, the American air base at Alconbury was very active, whereas RAF Wittering was quite inactive. So we chose a former dairy near Wittering, which was a listed 19th-century building, in a small hamlet between Peterborough and Stamford. As it turned out, Alconbury was shut down in the years following, whereas Wittering housed the Harrier vertical take-off jets, and it proved to be extremely noisy when they were practising hovering not far from our house!

In any case, we moved into the house, which had plenty of room and a large garden. There were ten other children of similar ages living in the hamlet and our boys spent much playtime with them, particularly in the many acres of woodland by the hamlet.

Shortly after we moved in, we were joined by a full-time nanny called Emma, who lived a few miles away in Peterborough.

All three boys attended the local primary school, and then Stamford School. So, Christine and I believed that the boys' life was good. I felt Christine and I were working well to support the family, albeit with a lot of help from Emma. Christine loved her job, I was building up a company nearly an hour's commute away, and so the children's care and welfare during the week was left almost entirely in the very capable hands of Emma. As I saw it, weekends were family time, when we would take them to school sports such as rugby (which I grew to hate due to the visits to A&E with an injured child).

I have come to realise that I was kidding myself at this time, wanting us to appear a 'happy' family from the outside while our drinking and focus on our work lives meant that the boys didn't get as much love and attention as they needed. This realisation was driven home recently when I talked to Emma about this time. The next chapter provides a glimpse of life at the Old Dairy as she experienced it. It is a powerful testimony and a very painful read all these years later, looking back on that time.

For a while, I thought all was going well with Camdata. However, there were some fatal flaws in how we ran the company. For one thing, we were unaware of the financial ratio critical to sustaining a business: customer acquisition cost versus lifetime value. If it costs more to find and retain a customer than the money one can make from that customer, the business will quickly fail. We had far too many one-off projects, either directly with a customer or with their customers. I didn't know how to calculate the contribution of a customer to the profit of a company and our non-executive finance director was a senior accountant and had not been entrepreneurial. We would probably have made more profit if we had turned down some customers and concentrated on others.

There were two other factors which led to Camdata's demise. One was that our bookkeeper, who used an early PC-based accounting package, was posting purchased components to 'stock' and not to 'cost of manufacture'. This meant that it looked like we were making good profits, but it was all due to an accounting error. She was inexperienced, and I blame myself and our board for not training her.

I remember clearly suddenly realising that although we were apparently making good profits, the company often had to increase its bank overdraft and had started factoring customer invoices. This means selling the invoices to a bank which would advance the money for a fee. In other words, the profit and loss account and the balance sheet were out of step. One said we were making profits and the other showed increasing borrowing.

We brought in an external consultant to improve and oversee our processes, we repriced projects and products, I stopped using my company car, made three staff redundant and the orders (guaranteed profitable now) flooded in. We had strong product-market fit, but with a hole in the balance sheet, supported by debt.

And how much was that debt costing? Interest base rates in 1989 were around 15%, so we were paying close to 20% per year for our debt pile. At its peak this debt was over £500,000 (at 2023 prices), and the interest payment alone was the equivalent of employing many staff.

This was acceptable, until the economy crashed. We would normally have an order book of around six to eight weeks, which in late 1989/early 1990 increased to nearly six months – a very comfortable situation. But the big UK corporates had switched off capital expenditure in the summer of 1989. This didn't hit us until about nine months later, as the effect took time to filter through and we were always just a small part of the many projects we were undertaking. We had not built a maintenance or service income and were entirely dependent on equipment sales. With increasing frustration and worry, the sales team could not close any new orders while we worked through the existing order book. The company was still profitable but we all had an impending sense of doom.

We decided to outsource all our manufacturing to a sub-contracted manufacturer, Richard, to whom we had given his first order when he set up his business. He also took over our leased industrial unit in another village, all our production staff and stock, so we cut overheads and had a completely flexible supply chain. So, where did this leave the family finances? I stopped taking a salary in January 1990, I had already stopped using my company car and we relied on the little savings we had plus Christine's good income from environmental consulting. Meanwhile, I was working even longer hours mainly helping the sales team try to close orders. This was reflected in longer absences from home and less time as a family.

By this time, I was pretty stressed. My longer-term dreams were falling apart and operating the business was getting more and more stressful. I took to immersing myself in books, and read almost all of Stephen King's horror novels, which were pure escapism. This was better than drinking myself to oblivion, which occasionally happened, but much less frequently than a few years later. Even so, this was a difficult time which would soon start to take its toll on the family. Christine travelled extensively for work and so was also absent from the family home a great deal. Slowly but surely, our relationship started to erode, and the care of the boys fell almost entirely to our nanny.

Chapter 5
Emma's Story

A glimpse into life at the Old Dairy

Interview with Emma, who was our nanny from August 1988 until September 1992. PC is Peter Cowley, EB is Emma Belgrove.

PC: So you found the job through an advert?

EB: Yes, sole charge of the three boys. When I came, both you and Christine were very focused on work. The hours on the contract were 8:40 till 4:45, but it was always much more than that. The communication was sort of three-way, because there was the communication between you and Christine, and then there was what Christine had asked me to do, but then she would go away and you didn't really know or seem to care what was agreed. It was just a little bit tricky. So yes, often the boys came and stayed at mine.

PC: We all had mobile phones then, didn't we?

EB: It was early stages – I had one fitted in my car. Often you were meant to be back at six or seven and you didn't come back at that time. It was always hard for me to make plans outside of work because I would inevitably have to cancel them. The boys would ask what time you were coming back or "when's Mummy coming back?" When you did return, you often smelt of alcohol and you never apologised for being late. You were both very focused on work. You both loved the boys, but it was not a conventional sort of setup. There was a lack of physical affection between you and Christine, but a void of affection and nurture towards the children. You both put work and travel before the children. I would provide the hugs, routine, stability and encouragement. I would always tell them I loved them and how proud I was of them.

PC: Christine worked from home until 1991. Then I had to work from home, didn't I?

EB: There was a period that you were both working from home. You were in the barn and Christine was in her office. And at that point, your relationship with Christine was quite fractured and basically you were both sticking your heads in the sand. I think that was the issue. You were just living separate lives. I felt in the middle, often the go-between, whilst trying to protect the children from any angst between you two.

PC: Apart from holidays.

EB: Apart from holidays. Christine was working a lot and she would drink quite a bit – she'd have her red wine and have her papers all out in her office. I remember walking in and she'd be having one of those days where her whole office was covered with papers, busy filing. When you came home from work you would disappear to your office. I'd continue to give the boys their tea, bath them, get them ready for bed, help with their homework and read them a bedtime story. I was the one who would attend the boys' class assemblies, concerts, fêtes. I taught them to swim, took them to after-school clubs, parties, visiting Santa's grotto, all those sorts of things. Sometimes, I felt sad that you and Christine were missing out on seeing some of their developmental milestones. I saw Alan's first steps, Ian's first independent swimming strokes and Matt's first day at school, to name but a few. But I felt I was the lucky one! I loved the responsibility, the feeling of making a difference to their little lives and the love they gave me.

PC: And so 4:45 became 7:45 and later.

EB: Often later. Sometimes, quite a lot of the time, I'd take them and they'd stay at mine, or sometimes I'd stay over at yours. I just loved being with them. My plan when I first got the job was to work one year. But I fell in love with the boys so much, I couldn't leave them, I was so attached to them. I think in some aspects both you and Christine were great employers, even though the communication wasn't great between the two of you. For a nanny, it was ideal in some respects, because I had some friends that were nannies that had restrictive employers, wanting them to do certain things, in a certain way, or they wouldn't pay for activities or overtime. Christine was great. She would say whatever I needed to do with the boys, I could do. She always paid me for every minute I worked and she trusted me, you both did. And I was very honoured to have that role.

Five years is a long time, all day, every day. The boys were very resilient and very good at being able to adapt between different adult roles and rules. When I was there, we'd have certain rules, and then when I would go, often you and Christine would still be working, and the boys had free rein! I remember one day leaving work and they'd got sticks. I was saying: "be careful of your eyes, mind your eyes." I remember it was time for me to go, and you and Christine were at home and I was thinking, well, they're both there, they are responsible for them now! When I came back the following day, one of the boys had been poked in the eye with a stick, and I thought, I should have stayed. Often I worried terribly about leaving them. I knew when the boys were left with either of you they would usually be left to roam freely at the Old Dairy.

PC: But you've got lots of great memories, haven't you?

EB: Great memories. Just the best, absolute best.

PC: So you stayed until Alan went to Barnack School full time, basically from when he was a baby, an infant, and then to playgroup and then going on to Barnack.

EB: The day I left, it was really hard because I didn't want to leave, but obviously Alan was going to school full time, so there wasn't really a role in the day for me. The day I left, I was in such a state, I was heartbroken. I actually felt a physical pain when I left. And I said to my mum, I don't know how I can go through these emotions, because although they were your children, they actually felt part of me, and they have always felt part of me, always. As you can see from all the photos, I absolutely adore them, still do think of them daily. I've got a picture of the boys on my dressing table now, so every morning they're with me. Although they're not my children, they feel like part of me.

Chapter 6
The Lost Decade

I don't regret many things in life, and I make it a rule not to, but I do regret not spending more time with the boys as they were growing up. The truth is that during their younger years, I was consumed with building Camdata and then keeping it afloat. The second half of 1990 became very tough for the business. Cash flow was very tight, we made more staff redundant, we employed a consultancy firm to try and raise external capital and got close to doing so with one of our customers, but they couldn't justify the cost of stabilising the company financially. With fewer staff and steady but lower sales, we could operate, but we had built up a lot of very expensive bank debt and a long list of creditors.

Some of my staff had managed to find other jobs, although that was difficult as the UK recession deepened, but for those who remained, we ensured we paid the salaries early every month.

Christmas 1990 was no fun. I was internalising too much of my worry about the future of the company, keeping it from our staff and my family, which is common for CEOs when they go through really difficult times.

The crunch came in February 1991, when we realised external funding was impossible and that supplier creditor pressure was too strong, so we contacted a liquidator for advice. As it turned out, we appointed them less than an hour before our remarkably patient bank tried to appoint a receiver. Christine and I had given a Personal Guarantee and a second charge on our house (which meant that we could not sell the house without paying them back) for £60,000. The bank wanted us to increase that to

£180,000 (from £170,000 to over £500,000 in 2023 prices), which was the combined overdraft and mortgage on the Old School. Signing that could easily have led to personal bankruptcy, so we refused.

As a result, the bank tried to take over the running of the company solely for their benefit. This meant we would lose control of the company. By appointing a liquidator ourselves, we also lost control, but we could at least try to ensure that trade creditors would potentially receive some of their money back.

Our Production Director Phil could see the end was nigh and had arranged to set up a new business selling bare Printed Circuit Boards using external investors, if Camdata failed. For myself, I soon obtained some IT consultancy work with one of Christine's customers.

The next few weeks were spent ensuring as high a return as possible for the creditors by selling some of the company's Intellectual Property, collecting debts, finding a buyer for the Old School (it was bought by the person who was doing our manufacturing, Richard, who is still in the building thirty years later), selling stock and assets and bidding up the prices, ensuring the employees were paid their redundancy pay, and many other procedures that accompany liquidation.

Camdata failing was a huge loss for me. I had let down staff, customers, suppliers, I had lost my dream (and my source of income) and I even felt a little sorry for the bank!

I realise now that I had started grieving for the loss some months before, while continuing to fight to survive until the end, and that after it failed, I found a sense of relief. By chance, I even went on our local BBC TV channel the very afternoon we appointed the liquidator. I had been invited to share my views of the economy, having been chosen because Camdata was in the then Prime Minister (John Major's) constituency.

My processing of grief unfortunately is a continuing theme in my life. In this case, I was grieving the loss of a future I had projected for myself, the loss of all the hard work and effort I had put into the business and the loss of part of my identity as a successful entrepreneur. Still, this was very different from grieving for a loved one, because unlike a human (unless one believes in reincarnation), a company can be reborn.

And that is exactly what happened in the end. With the help of a friend, Gerry, I put in an offer for the assets of the business, a process that is all too common nowadays and is called a 'pre-pack' or Phoenix. This process was very tough in those days, to prevent unscrupulous business owners from cynically shedding creditors and then restarting.

I created a trading entity, but could not use the name Camdata, so chose Axon Consultants, by glancing through a dictionary and liking the connection with the brain (an axon conducts electrical impulses within the brain and between the brain and the rest of the body). This had unlimited liability and I soon formed a company, Axxon Communication Limited, which earned me a heavy letter from Exxon (the global oil company) saying they had the global rights to any commercial name with two consecutive letters X. I wrote back that I had no intention of competing with them, and heard no more.

Gerry had bought the assets, as I could not, although there was never any suggestion that the directors of Camdata had done anything fraudulent.

So I was in business again. Some customers had bought intellectual property from us and hence no longer needed Camdata, some had found other suppliers, but the majority were very pleased that they could continue working with me. My suppliers, of course, were cautious and I had to pay cash for all deliveries for at least a year. Richard, who'd bought the Old School premises, continued to do all the manufacturing and I paid him back for all the losses he'd had from Camdata.

Aged thirty-five, I was working from home in a converted barn next to the Old Dairy, and this had two consequences, almost immediately. The new company was very profitable as it had almost no overheads, no debt and I was charging the same amount as before, so I bought an ex-demo red (!) sports car, the first of what I call my several 'mid-life crisis' cars. But there were simply not enough hours in the day to do the sales and the project processing and the accounts. One very loyal employee, Pete, joined me, working from the same premises as Richard, in his home village and staying with me for twenty-five years. To reduce my working hours, I employed an operations director, Kevin, who married our nanny Emma a couple of years later.

The money was coming in, I was a good salesman and also knew how to buy to optimise profit, but I had the little issue of the £60,000 Personal Guarantee (PG) hanging over me. We had no intention of moving house, so the second charge was not an issue, but the bank had lost about £100,000 – offset by the actions of Phil and myself in realising assets for the liquidator, and through Richard buying the Old School – and the bank wanted the Personal Guarantee back!

This took a few years, mainly for two reasons. First, although Camdata was making money and Christine was earning from her consultancy, the debt was clearly mine and not ours and with mortgage interest rates over 15%, cash was tight. Second, the bank seemed to want to negotiate. I suspect they had written the debt down by a large amount, and any money was better than none. They knew that if they pressed too hard, they would force us to sell our house.

So they were patient and called me to their offices once or twice a year. I remember wearing casual clothes without a jacket to give the impression things were tight, which they certainly were. Whether it had the desired effect on the bank, I have no idea.

After about three years of paying them instalments, they agreed on a settlement figure of about half the amount they sought. Nowadays it is common for a bank to sell such a debt to a collection agency for perhaps 10% of the full value, but a collection agency's tactics can be more aggressive.

At this point, we had spare cash and decided to convert part of the barn into a large living room, two more bedrooms and a kids' playroom.

But times were getting tougher within my marriage. Christine was travelling overseas more and more, and would be away ten to fifteen times a year, often for a fortnight. Her work as an environmental consultant was interesting and a very important part of her identity. The income meant we could maintain a large house, three boys at private school, a full-time nanny and foreign holidays. However, when she came back from her travels, she would struggle to settle back into home life, seeking refuge in her office, where she would work late and then sleep in the living room. We were inexorably drifting apart, gradually losing interest in each other, no longer able to communicate. Our drinking was getting worse, particularly mine, as I was on a steady but inexorable path to alcoholism, and we were leading mostly separate lives.

As it happened, Christine had gone into business with another environmental consultant, Dave, and they formed a covert relationship. This came to light when one day I noticed a hotel invoice on her desk which showed that they were sharing a room. I questioned Christine about this and she said it was to save costs and work late into the night. To support this, she said that Dave had just left his wife for another woman and would therefore hardly be having an affair with her, Christine. She suggested I meet Dave's wife to hear this directly from her. So I did, and Dave's wife confirmed that it was all true. This helped stave off my doubts for a while, as I just couldn't believe that Christine would be having an affair with a man who'd just left his wife for another woman, although this is exactly what was happening. Later I would find that Dave had very complex relationships with several women at once. Some months later we went for marriage guidance counselling, which was interesting yet unfruitful, partly as Christine didn't turn up for the first three weeks, due to a project that she was doing for the World Bank in Africa.

*   *   *   *   *

By this time, my drinking had become so problematic that it was a battle putting off the first drink of the day until as late as possible. This internal craving would distract me from whatever I should have been doing. If there was any alcohol left from the night before or my shaking hands were making teeth-cleaning difficult, that first drink could happen before breakfast. But whenever it happened, the day would then only go downhill until sleep took over.

I thought it was normal to hide alcohol, to deny my drinking, to drink alone and secretly, to have blackouts and to drink before breakfast to prevent the shakes.

In 1994, I had an epileptic fit on my parents' kitchen floor. I had drunk heavily on Sunday and on Monday morning faced the choice between having a drink to stop the shaking and ruining the day, or not drinking and trying to have a reasonable working day. I chose not to drink, which resulted in the fit, thereby ruining many other people's days in the process. I was taken to our local hospital and I remember clearly reading the form at the end of the bed (long before electronic patient record systems), which simply said 'Alcoholic'. But how could that be? I knew I drank a lot but I was not an alcoholic. As it turned out, that word on the form let me off the hook in one respect. In many cases, people lose their driving licence for a year if they have an unexplained fit. I kept my licence, as the reason for the fit was clinically clear.

After a couple of days in hospital, and with some pressure from Christine and my parents, I checked into St Andrew's

Healthcare, a mental health facility in Northampton, for a week. I found it a very supportive environment, but it was costly and I didn't really know why I was there. There was one big positive outcome: I had weekly follow-up sessions with a psychiatrist and began to understand in an intellectual way what addiction was. However, denial is strong, and I didn't think the word addiction applied to me. So, I soon went back to my old ways – perhaps, illustrating the difference between my understanding addiction intellectually but not emotionally.

My drinking got very bad again towards the end of 1994, to the point where I knew that my alcohol consumption was unmanageable and I decided to undergo a five-week rehabilitation program over that Christmas. This time I chose The Retreat in York, where one of my uncles had been treated for his own alcohol addiction. I had made a more conscious choice to undergo treatment, which meant that in principle there was more chance that it would work. People can and do force interventions on alcoholics, and such interventions can work on rare occasions, but whether they do or not depends on the alcoholic.

Strange as it may sound, I enjoyed my time in York. I moved our family black Labrador up with me (in kennels), took my car, saw local Yorkshire friends, and met and befriended a fascinating long-term resident of The Retreat, Lord Bicester, who had been there for seven years. Angus, as he asked to be called, was there for other reasons and, like me, could come and go as he pleased, provided he attended therapy sessions. Angus introduced me to betting on the horses – I was forty and had never been in a betting shop – and to some of his friends who had large country estates in the area.

Post-treatment support was at York. This was a very long round trip from Stamford and well before video consultations, so not ideal. However, another patient introduced me to his personal therapist, Vicky, who lived locally to me in Peterborough. This turned out to be a much more important piece in the jigsaw puzzle of how I made life changes that helped me to stay sober.

As it turned out, what I had learned in The Retreat in York 'worked' for only five months. During this time, what I was doing is classed as being a 'dry drunk' by AA. This is also called white-knuckling, which means staying sober through sheer willpower alone. Put bluntly, I was not drinking alcohol but still thinking and behaving as if I was, just without the physical effects of alcohol. In other words, I had not addressed the issues that had originally caused my drinking to become an addiction.

I thought I was doing well, but – and unfortunately when one is addicted there are always 'buts' – I had been to a dinner event with my bank manager and drunk a glass of wine. I had driven there and knew I had to drive back, so there was a good reason in the back of my mind not to drink much. I thought that after five months off alcohol I was strong enough to drink socially and this seemed a good opportunity to start. Surely one glass of wine would do no harm? How incredibly wrong I was. Wine became spirits and within a few weeks I was heading back to square one. It took me another five years to finally enter proper recovery, in March of 2000, a recovery that is still ongoing. In the AA system, one is never 'cured' from alcoholism, but, hopefully, always 'in recovery'.

Vicky was probably the best therapist I have ever had in terms of our relationship, the tools she used and the outcome of the therapy. In her sessions, I worked out that Christine and I were in an unhealthy mutually dependent dynamic, that relied on me continuing drinking. Christine needed me to do this (although obviously not to dangerous levels) so that I wouldn't have a life of my own and could therefore be relied upon to be at home with the children, even if I wasn't actually 'there' for them very much at the times when I was drunk (being 'there' was the role of the nannies). This meant she was free to travel for work and personal reasons. From my point of view, I wanted this setup to continue because I needed her to be a mother to our children, to bring in money and perhaps also to appear to the outside world to be a 'happy family'.

At the start of 1995, we were joined by a full-time live-in nanny called Dawn. The kids loved her. Christine gave Dawn a credit card and told her to use it for whatever the boys needed. Dawn bought their clothes and spent her first year decorating their bedrooms. Like Emma, she did a lot with the boys, taking them to their judo and piano, and to eat fish and chips on Fridays. It was a bit of baptism of fire for Dawn. Aged just twenty-three, she had come straight out of university and teacher training and did not feel geared up for a household with drinking and divided parents. However, she focused on looking after the boys and she formed a particularly strong bond with Alan. She remembers being at the Old Dairy many times at weekends, when Christine was away, and that my parents, who lived next door at that time, also helped a great deal. Alan in particular spent a lot of time at my parents' house.

I got on with Dawn well. When Christine was away and when I wasn't drinking, I spent a lot of evenings in the family home either working or watching TV with her and the boys. I would take the boys on foreign holidays and Dawn would come, too. We would all really enjoy those holidays.

It became increasingly clear to me, to the point of it being undeniable, that Christine and Dave were in fact having an affair. In mid-1995, with my therapist Vicky's support, I told Christine that the marriage was not working for me and that it was over. I just could not cope with her having another relationship outside our marriage. As Princess Diana once famously said: 'There were three of us in this marriage, so it was a bit crowded.' That was our situation, too, and I realised I could not go on like that.

We called the boys together in the kitchen to tell them we were going to divorce, and we were both crying. The boys didn't say very much and then just got on with whatever they had been doing. This could, of course, just be one of the ways in which children initially respond to events of this kind in their lives. Or maybe it wasn't such news for them and they had seen it coming. They had Dawn, they had a very strong group of friends in the hamlet and each other, but it pains me to think of the parental love and support they were missing.

Christine and I then visited a mediation service to work through childcare and finances, and then the situation got even more complicated.

Much to Dawn's understandable annoyance, her mother, Wendy, left her comfortable job in Peterborough and decided also to become a nanny. Dawn was trying to strike out on her own in life and felt her mum was dogging her footsteps. Wendy's attempt at nannying was a complete disaster, resulting in her walking out after a week or so, and because she had rented out her flat, she stayed with us for a couple of nights. She and I formed a relationship, which was tricky for Dawn. I was obviously on the rebound, and Wendy had been looking for a relationship for a while. My confidence in affairs of the heart had taken a blow, so it was a great feeling to be wanted. I had felt starved of love and affection, and Wendy was very happy to oblige. There was also the element of her wanting to be part of Dawn's life somehow. Wendy was very patient, except when I was drinking. After the five months of being dry, I had started to drink again, but my drinking was much more controlled and we used to spend a few nights a week together.

I had a companion and someone I could love and be loved by. However, the boys were a little confused and Dawn struggled with her own relationship with her mother until Wendy broke up with me, a year-and-a-half later, when my drinking finally got too much for her.

During this time, I had a choice of accommodation: the family home if Christine was away and Dawn off duty, or the house next to my parents', just yards from the marital home, where my parents kindly allowed me to convert the upstairs into my bedroom and living room and Wendy's flat until we broke up.

In 1997, I bought a house near the centre of Stamford and near the kids' school. I saw a lot of the boys as I commonly worked from home. Dawn was still working for Christine as the boys' nanny, and she would often bring them to mine after school. After Dawn left in 1999 it was an unstable time for the boys, as they couldn't really get on with any nannies after Dawn.

I regard the entire decade from 1990 to 2000 as my 'lost decade'. First in 1990 my business failed, then in 1995 my marriage imploded, leading to final separation shortly after a brief spell of sobriety on my part. The following years were a bit of a blur as my alcoholic dependency strengthened, although I was running Camdata, doing the first year of an Open University degree in Psychology, plus an A level in Law. I spent time with the kids and with a succession of girlfriends until I met a woman called Margaret at a singles club in Stamford, with whom I had a relationship both as an alcoholic and later also in recovery.

My life looked okay from the outside. I had a lodger who I went into business with. I had an active social life with friends, many of whom drank, but not to excess. I was what is commonly regarded as a high-functioning drunk and I managed to keep the business running with the help and support of staff. I had a part-time Office and Marketing Manager, who helped me by answering the phone when I was slurring my speech and drove me to customer meetings if I couldn't. I generated enough income to live, I was helping a couple of charities, I went on foreign holidays and I had a semblance of a relationship with my children and parents, albeit on their terms. All of this enabled me to fool myself into thinking that I didn't really have a problem.

Until I hit rock bottom.

Chapter 7

Rock Bottom

In early September 1999 I went to Scotland with Matt, who was fifteen at the time, to climb Ben Nevis. What happened next is something that I am more ashamed of than almost anything else in my life. Showing the madness of the practising alcoholic, I drank while driving all the way up to Scotland. Matt decided I was too drunk, so he confiscated my car keys and rang a friend in Stamford. The friend then contacted my parents, who drove up to rescue Matt. It was agreed that I would have the car keys back and carry on. My parents and Matt would stay the night in a hotel and take him home the next day.

The next day, I mixed half a litre of gin with orange juice to disguise the alcohol, which I drank as I successfully climbed and then descended the highest mountain in the UK. Back in Fort William, I jumped into the car in order to drive some or all of the 450 miles back home. I remember little of the next few hours apart from the fact that I got lost in Glasgow (this was before satnavs). Two hours later, I stopped on a side road to relieve myself and got the car stuck on the verge. A kind passer-by helped me push the car back onto the tarmac and also, as it turned out, rang the police to say I was drunk behind the wheel. Without me noticing, a marked police car started to follow me, and stayed with me for many miles down the M6 motorway, until I stopped at a service area near the Lake District.

The police car parked next to my car and the officer beckoned me over. I sat in the passenger seat of his car as he told me that I hadn't committed any traffic offences so he could not stop me any earlier. I remember to my embarrassment uttering the words "It's a fair cop." After drink-driving for many years, I had been caught, miraculously without having injured myself or anyone else, and I felt I was getting my due come-uppance. I'd had a few close shaves – for instance, just before Christmas the previous year. The police were stopping everyone and looking at drivers, but not breathalysing them unless they suspected them of being over the limit. I had been drinking in the car, but looked respectable and drove a 'nice' car, so they made the assumption I wouldn't be a drink-driver.

This time round, I was breathalysed and found to be more than three times over the limit, taken to the police station, breathalysed again, charged and placed in a police cell. I had behaved, I believe, in an exemplary fashion throughout, politely and cooperatively, so I was allowed out (without my car keys) to stay in a local pub for the night and told I could have my car back as soon as I blew a clear breath sample. The pub had a room, and I then did what any alcoholic would do and asked for a pint of beer. And another.

After a poor night's sleep, I got my car back at 6am after passing a breathalyser test, and rang Margaret, who, together with my parents, had had a terrible night as they knew I was driving and suspected I was drunk. I had not been able to contact them for over twelve hours because my mobile phone was still in the confiscated car.

As the offence took place in Cumbria, I was summoned to appear in court in Appleby a few weeks later, on the 23rd of September. I was advised by both the court and my solicitor to travel up by train as there was little chance of leaving the court building with my driving licence intact. I caught the train up, drinking all the way and into the evening, and stayed at a local pub. The court hearing was mid-morning and I was definitely hungover and gently shaking (the so-called DTs – Delirium Tremens). I tried my best to look respectably dressed in a jacket and tie and had a local solicitor representing me. The fine was hefty and the sentence was twenty-four months' loss of my driving licence, because my blood alcohol level was so high.

Before I had travelled up to Appleby, my neighbour and friend, Philip, had volunteered to act as my driver during the ban that we knew was coming as a result of the court case, partly for some income, and partly as he loved cars and I had a comfortable although somewhat old BMW which he adored driving. I bought him a chauffeur's peaked cap, which he wore with amused pride.

A few days before the court hearing, he suggested I attend an AA meeting. We discussed it and I agreed that that would be a good idea. So, on my return from the court case, he collected me from Peterborough station and drove me straight to my first meeting.

There I spoke the following words:

"I'm Peter, I'm an alcoholic."

It was the first time I said these words, which I would repeat again and again at hundreds more AA meetings over the next two years.

That first meeting was a terrible shock. With the group, I listened to a well-dressed, well-spoken man of about my age tell the group that he had been sober for several years, but that, when drinking, if he couldn't get out of his house to buy more alcohol, he used to drink his own vomit, because it had alcohol in it. This was so extreme that I convinced myself (in my befuddled view) I was not 'like that', so that actually I could not possibly be an alcoholic. I clung to this view for another six months, until I went to rehab for the third and finally successful visit.

This meant that unlike probably everyone else in the room, I was not in fact in recovery. Everyone is welcome at an AA meeting if they are experiencing problems with their drinking and want to do something about it. But I was still drinking, and alcohol was still ruining my health, my relationships, my finances and threatening my life. As soon as I got home that evening,

I went straight out to our local wine shop and bought three bottles of white wine for £10 – I doubt there was much left in the morning. Addiction is closely associated with denial (which, as AA says, is not a river in Africa!) and there is absolutely no doubt that I was in denial.

The AA has a particular view on the term 'alcoholic' (it has views on many other things, too). I was taught that one can never call someone else an alcoholic or accuse another person of being an alcoholic, but that instead the word is reserved for members of AA when talking about themselves. It is described within AA as a physical compulsion coupled with a mental obsession which has led to negative effects on our health and relationships.

Many therapists in the years after I entered sobriety asked me when I felt I had started to drink alcoholically. I used to reply that I had been given 'permission' to drink during the day when I found a cold wine spritzer on Christine's desk at 8am after she had taken the children to school. I felt she was encouraging or at least enabling me, but blaming her is both unfair and unjust. My denial was so strong that I latched on to any excuse, whereas what I should have done instead was take responsibility for my own alcoholism, and of course challenge her drinking.

Examples of behaviour that I thought acceptable included using a towel over my mouth to prevent vomiting when I took the first drink of the day, sometimes before breakfast, in order to stop my hands shaking.

How can any rational person take that as acceptable behaviour, whilst knowing that the day was now ruined? As an alcoholic, one drink always leads to another. One of the AA sayings is that an alcoholic will never be able to control which the last drink of the day will be. Only sleep or unconsciousness will define that. Probably with a half-empty glass of one's drink of choice by the bed.

While I was a so-called high-functioning drunk, as described earlier, over an hour of each day would be spent 'hunting' for alcohol. I had seven shops in Stamford where I bought my alcohol, making weekly visits to each, and knew numerous pubs, so that I could live in the illusion that the shopkeepers or pub landlords didn't know I had a drink problem. Three bottles of white wine for £10 (£20 in 2023) was a normal day. Years later, Alan worked in an off-licence in a village near Cambridge and he talked of a well-known author who used to visit every day to buy the same quantity of alcohol.

I could and did have days without drinking any alcohol. I remember gradually reducing my drinking over the days before an event when I needed to be sober – perhaps an important customer meeting or a day with my parents and kids. However, such a plan would invariably crumble under stress. For instance, when I really wanted to go to the funeral of a very good friend from school called Tony, who had died in his early forties of leukaemia, I couldn't trust myself to be sober enough that day to drive there.

So as to have a very solid reason to not pick up a drink during the day, I took up amateur dramatics, not on stage but on the lighting desk, as I had done as a schoolboy. The idea was that this would stop me drinking in the day, because I would then be letting down the cast and technical staff in the evening. This worked really well, until the first night.

Wednesday the 22nd of March 2000 and the first night of the play, *The Night of the Iguana*. I have no clue what made me pick up that first drink but, why should I? I am Peter and I am an alcoholic. I remember none of the play, but luckily my lighting mentor was in the technical box doing the sound and overseeing me.

The next day, I woke and, although we had the second night of the play coming up, I picked up a drink again. Philip came round to see how I was and I stumbled on the garden path and fell, just missing a boot mud scraper with two vertical prongs that could easily have killed or seriously wounded me. I don't remember this myself, but Philip told me later that I had said I would rather be dead than continue as an alcoholic. Philip realised that this may be a rock bottom for me and gently convinced me that it might be time to attend a rehabilitation clinic again. I was in shock about having just had a near-death experience, and as it happened, I was in a particular state between sober denial and drunken stupidity. I said yes.

Between us we sourced and rang a number of clinics and found a place to start that day at a Priory Clinic in Nottingham. Many people have heard of the Priory in London where celebrities go, including Amy Winehouse, Kate Moss and Eric Clapton, but the Priory also has a number of smaller clinics around the country. We needed a referral, which my GP duly supplied. The Priory said I should arrive drunk so that I didn't have an epileptic fit en route. My sister, Sue, was living with me, so she went out and bought a bottle of gin, of which I consumed about half, before Philip drove me the fifty miles or so to Nottingham. I had had plenty of time to pack, although I wasn't really in much of a state to concentrate.

I rang Margaret, my parents and the kids (sixteen, fourteen and twelve at the time) as we travelled. I was filled with a sense of relief, trepidation and excitement. I had no clue at that point that 18:05 on Thursday the 23rd of March 2000 would mark the last alcoholic drink that I voluntarily consumed. My breathalyser reading when I arrived was over five times the UK drink-drive limit and I had not had a fit.

My respect and love for Philip deepened. He had taken me to my first AA meeting after I had my driving licence taken away, and by the time he took me to the Priory, I had been to about thirty AA meetings. I knew something about their methods, I had my own sponsor called Mick, and I knew that this day needed to be known as my 'rock bottom', if I and I alone was to enter sobriety for the rest of my life.

Chapter 8

The Beginning of the End

It was tough at the Priory. The first few days were tolerable, but the realisation soon dawned that I was going to have to build a new life, lose friends who were just drinking buddies and make new ones, and work through the AA programme. The Priory works on the AA 12-step principle, unlike the other two rehabs I had visited. I believe it was a cocktail of luck, fate and my soon-to-be-recognised 'higher power' that 'chose' the Priory. The first two steps of the 12-step programme are: admitting that you are powerless over alcohol and your life has become unmanageable, and then: coming to believe that a power greater than yourself can restore you to sanity. When founded in 1935, the institution called the higher power God, but that has changed over time to be 'a power greater than ourselves', which can be anything you regard as such, be it Buddha, the universe or love, that you feel can help your recovery. I arrived at AA as a technologist and engineer, so I strongly believe in science, but I learned to become comfortable with the concept of a 'higher power'.

On arrival at the Priory, I said farewell to Philip and then was in a small sick bay area for two or three nights to go through withdrawal. I was dosed up to prevent an epileptic fit, but that didn't stop the tremors. Even with two hands, getting a cup or glass from the table to my lips required huge concentration and invariably led to some spillage.

The clinic has beds for about twenty-five people. Some self-pay (like me), some are funded via their employer (for instance the NHS and the American military), some via relatives (especially the younger heroin addicts) and some via local authorities. About two thirds of the patients (although we often referred to ourselves as inmates) had alcohol as their 'drug of choice' and a third were addicted to illegal (or sometimes legal) substances, with of course some overlap. The expectation was that you stayed there for twenty-eight days, following a programme based on group work on the premises and local AA/NA (Narcotics Anonymous) meetings most evenings. We had regular individual sessions with the qualified clinical staff as well.

I compared it to the Eagles' 'Hotel California' song – 'you can check out any time you like, but you can never leave' – although clearly for the opposite reasons. In our case we could never leave until we had completed the AA step one: 'We admitted we were powerless over alcohol – that our lives had become unmanageable.' Although the front gate was always open to a main road, which had shops and pubs selling alcohol, we were told we could not walk through it to buy a paper until we had completed step one, otherwise we would be expelled. This did of course happen, mostly with those coming off heroin, where the detoxification process was very much more painful than with alcohol. We observed this with almost every new drug addict. They called it 'roasting'.

As part of step one of the Priory programme, you write down goals. For me, the first two were 1) stay alive and 2) improve relationships with parents, kids, girlfriend, friends. There were another eight, to do with transitioning between the alcoholic and non-alcoholic phases of my life and sustaining my recovery, down to 7) stop spending £4,000 a year (£8,500 in today's money) on booze and 8) spread the gospel about the Priory technique and try to guide my children into not emulating my problem. Step one took about a week and although the process is defined by the clinic, for the most part help came from those more advanced on their journeys at the Priory. I have a huge amount of time and respect for group work, because of this. Of course I could not relate to every member of the group, but for those of us newbies who stuck it out (perhaps 75%) the 'seniors' provided huge encouragement, until we became group seniors ourselves.

In the first few days, I formed a bond with three women who arrived around the same time as me. They styled themselves the 'three witches', which was completely tongue-in-cheek, as they were all extremely supportive and caring and we ended up journeying at about the same speed to around the same departure date.

There was no concept of weekdays, except that there was less staff at the weekend. The days were long. We'd have a 7am start followed by breakfast, then group and individual meetings all day and AA/NA in the evenings, with little time to relax and reflect and no chance to exercise. I also still had Camdata to run, and visits from Alan, Margaret and friends. Christine didn't think it was a good idea for the boys to see me in the Priory, but Alan was keen and arranged with Philip to visit me. Matt and Ian waited until I got home. My parents relocated from the hamlet of my ex-marital home back to Yorkshire whilst I was at the Priory, which meant I couldn't help them move and they couldn't or perhaps wouldn't visit me.

Possibly the most difficult step (step four) was the one where we each had to write as honest an account as possible of our life, which of our family and friends we had hurt, and how we had done so. In step five, this was shared out loud with the group and the tears would come not just from the relater but from most of the rest of the group as well. The life story I told the group makes very painful reading now, especially the last section which covers the period just before I came to the Priory. It details how I had blackouts while on holiday on my own with my three children in Iceland, how I let down girlfriend after girlfriend with drunken telephone calls and unreliability. I had relationship problems with Christine and with my children, who would not come to stay with me and if they did come to see me, would turn straight round and go back to their mum's if they found me drunk. I would forget things, speak tactlessly. I would lie about alcohol consumption and steal from neighbours. By this time everyone in my life knew – friends, family, business clients, staff. I had accidents, including falling onto a wall after a six-hour drinking session in the pub and giving myself a black eye, and lots of bruising because I was forever stumbling around bumping into things. I guess the only slight positives during this time were that I was a friendly drunk, so didn't make any enemies, and that I never resorted to physical violence. I was extremely lucky to still have good and patient friends around me, and also that I was able to fund my addiction with a relatively successful business. Otherwise I would literally have been in the gutter.

In hindsight, I was a bit of an arsehole when I arrived. I didn't fit in with the group at all, initially, and I didn't join in properly. Deep down I knew I needed to, but on the surface my pride and my ego got in the way. I was arrogant, thinking that the group rules weren't for me, that I didn't need them, that I didn't really need to be there even. These things were gently pointed out to me, but it took at least a fortnight before my approach and level of humility fitted in with the others. A group in AA needs to work together following the 12-step concept, with all members behaving in the same way, which is beneficial for all involved. This is how its members can achieve long-term sobriety. Some never got to the point of being able to be part of the group in a genuine way, and some did on day one. I ended up staying there for twenty-five days and, like most others, during that time, I grew to love the group – we would all be very emotional when a member 'graduated' and left the Priory.

I became pretty desperate to get into my new sober life (one day at a time, of course) and to spend time once more with Margaret, my boys and parents, and to start work on the many plans that I had created. Not only that, but I was self-paying a few hundred pounds a day, which was a lot of money for me, so I did not want to extend my stay any longer than absolutely necessary. Of course, I could have walked out any time I wanted; the Priory may have felt like an open prison, but in fact we were accountable only to ourselves on whether to remain. When I expressed my desire to leave a few days early in one of my group sessions, the other group members were not keen, as they felt one had to stay the full course, but the Priory staff supported me. It was, and still is, extremely important to me to have as much control as possible over my own situation. In this case, it meant leaving the Priory when I felt I was ready, after step nine. Having written down everyone you've harmed (in step eight) you are ready to make amends, which of course, you can really only do outside the clinic. I also took the unusual step of asking for a full set of my clinical notes. This request was granted, and I received the notes, only partly redacted.

The group felt I was at great risk of relapse, that I would never 'make it' out there on my own, but nearly twenty-four years later, without a relapse, I have proved them wrong! However, leaving the Priory was really tough. I was leaving behind friends with whom I had shared everything and bonded in an intense way, and the outside world was a scary place where alcohol was available on every street corner.

Each group member writes a message to the person who is about to leave and of course they tend to be encouraging and positive. Apparently, I had been a good group member, supportive of others, positive and honest. I had self-confidence and a sense of humour, they said. However, other themes that recur in the messages were that I was in too much of a hurry, too concerned with what others thought of me, couldn't relax and focused on too many other things besides treatment (mainly my business and my mobile phone!). I had discovered that if I was bored, I was much more vulnerable to starting to drink, so part of my plan for staying in recovery had to revolve around finding activities, especially in the evenings, that would stave off this intellectual boredom. I planned to spend more time on bridge, amateur dramatics, time with friends, my children, my girlfriend, and also to attend AA meetings, of course.

The risk of falling off the wagon was illustrated strongly about two years later. I had kept in touch with all three of the so-called 'three witches' until one of them, who was a senior nurse, died suddenly of a ruptured aneurysm whilst at work at her hospital. I offered to drive the other two to her funeral in Grimsby, about five hours' return in the car. After we had stopped for a cup of tea on the A1, within minutes of resuming our journey, one of my passengers was suddenly very drunk. She had clearly had a drink in her handbag and consumed it secretly during our stop. This was a shocking reminder to the two of us who had stuck to the tea, of how very, very hard it was to stay sober in the real world. By the time we got to the funeral, she had sobered up, and we never confronted her about it.

On the day I left the Priory, the long-suffering Philip picked me up and drove me back to Stamford. Having 'escaped prison', the person who was going to guide and support me through the first days, weeks and months of being back in the outside world, with alcohol being available at every street corner, was Mick, my sponsor for the six months before I went into the Priory. I completely relied on him and the AA groups I attended – he was the first person to call if I felt tempted to pick up a drink. Mick had been sober for five years and I'd met him in one of the AA groups I attended before rehab. We lived close to each other and he offered to sponsor me.

I attended three or four AA meetings every week in local towns, including Stamford, to which I always travelled with other AA friends, as I was still banned from driving. There is an AA saying: '90 meetings in 90 days'. I didn't manage that, but I did attend as many as I could, listening to other stories, sharing my experiences and worries. I believe that I stayed sober during the following months purely because I had Mick and the AA support network around me.

A few months after I had come out of the Priory, I met a new member of this group who I shall call L. We got on well, and she asked me to be her AA sponsor. It is not generally recommended that males sponsor females or the other way around. Also, one normally has more time in recovery than I had at this point before becoming a sponsor, but despite this, I did agree, having talked it through with my own sponsor. Being a sponsor is a responsible role which involves being there for that person between and usually at AA meetings and guiding them through the 12-step programme. We spent some time together, which was difficult as she was still drinking. This didn't cause me any concern about my own sobriety but helping a tipsy or drunk person was beyond my experience. With support from her husband, she was admitted to the Priory in Nottingham. I had no role during this time, since the Priory was looking after her. After five weeks of rehab, the first thing she did after she came out was pick up a drink. I tried to help her in the subsequent months, but she died from her addiction whilst on vacation in France with her husband and three daughters.

Alcoholism is a terrible disease.

I thought long and hard about how I could have helped further, how I had failed her. In the end, I came to the conclusion that we simply cannot and should not take responsibility for another person's life and life choices. Of course, it is human to do so, but if you take on self-blame, guilt and regret, you can end up destroying your own life, without changing what happened or it doing anyone any good. This important lesson is one I took with me into the rest of my life, where I turned to it time and again as I lost family member after family member to addiction or mental health issues. It is a vital part of my coping mechanism – much easier said than done, but, unfortunately, practice makes possible.

* * * * *

Reintegration into 'normal' life after my five-week spell at The Retreat in York and twenty-five days at the Priory in Nottingham felt a bit like rejoining society after a short prison sentence, or so I imagine. I've only ever spent a few hours in an actual prison cell, of course, but that is how I think about it.

As mentioned before, my sister was living with me at the time I went into the Priory. She had been the one to go out and buy my last bottle of gin before Philip took me up to the Priory, so that I wouldn't fit due to withdrawal during the journey. But she was a heavy drinker herself and while in the Priory, I had realised that I needed her to live somewhere else to reduce temptation further and ensure there was never any alcohol in the house. So, Philip had helped to move her into a local B&B (paid for by me) before I came out in mid-April 2000. This did mean that I was alone in the house, a time of potentially extreme risk of relapse, so Philip suggested we have a short break with old friends near Munich. This would give me a change of scene, time with friends, a visit to a beer garden (definitely Philip's idea!) and a chance to drive a car.

Here I have to explain that in the weeks after my brief arrest in Appleby, but before being banned from driving in the court case a few weeks later, I had obtained an international driving licence. I knew I was going to lose my UK one, so this was a cunning plan to be able to continue driving, at least abroad. I also made a photocopy of my paper UK licence onto pink paper (no photograph, nor plastic card in those days). These two moves allowed me to hire and drive a car abroad. It was quite likely illegal, of course, but I tried not to think about that. I was used to driving a left-hand-drive vehicle on the continent from my time living in Germany, so I did all the driving. This was a really great time, with Philip, with friends, back in the area I had lived in for five years and enjoying German food, to which I am quite partial. I missed my kids and Margaret but it was for only a few days.

*   *   *   *   *

It took time for people close to me to believe and trust that I would not relapse. Maybe people still do think I will relapse? If I do, it certainly won't be due to using alcohol as an anaesthetic to reduce the pain I have endured, but I may do in the last days of my life – a thought I've had for many years, but doubt I will have the courage to enact.

Acceptance of my continuing recovery was especially slow in the case of my mother. Some years earlier, she had told me how selfish I was, and I had interpreted this as my alcohol-induced selfish behaviour. She was absolutely right, and I think it was several years before she trusted me when I said I hadn't had a drink since March 2000. Like most of the medical profession at that time, my father never accepted that alcoholism is a disease and that self-control is not enough to overcome it. However, he rapidly became more optimistic that I would remain sober. I'm very proud that I never had another drink in their lifetime (and still haven't had one!).

My children tested me for several months, by behaving as before and dropping by after school. School was just two minutes' walk away and previously they would go straight on to their mum's (another two minutes' walk) if I had been drinking, but they began to trust me and visited more and more often. In late 1999, Christine and I had sold the Old Dairy and she bought a house very close to mine and near the boys' school.

I spent three weeks in the USA with Alan, visiting my sister who had gone back to work in Connecticut, seeing the Niagara Falls, Chicago, Vancouver (where I vowed never to mountain bike again after a fall on an 'easy' run in Whistler) and New Orleans. In each location, we hired an open-top Mustang, which was a lot of fun, and I went to a very uplifting AA meeting in Seattle, the only one I attended outside the UK.

Although each boy had his own room in both my and their mum's houses, they all called their mum's house home until three weeks after our return from the USA, when Alan moved his home to mine, while continuing to visit his mum. He had accepted I was now reliably sober, offering a more stable home than his mum, who was still drinking. Both Alan and Ian were doing the same with their mum as they had done with me: if she was drunk they would leave her house and come to mine. Matt was sixteen and more independent, and he kept his home at his mum's. All three boys now were comfortable that I was reliable and really believed that I had stopped drinking.

About a year later, Ian also moved in with me, although the timing of his announcement was very painful for his mother. The three of us were in the school headteacher's office discussing Ian's behaviour and the possibility that he might fail his A levels. Towards the end of the meeting, without any warning, he announced he would move in with me and Alan. At the time, he told the headteacher that he thought I would support him more with his academic work, probably because he thought that's what the headteacher wanted to hear. It was actually more complicated than that, but I never definitively worked out whether it was because I would provide more support, or more freedom, or he wanted to avoid his mother's drinking, or a combination of these factors.

I rebuilt other friendships, had a so much better time with Margaret, who could trust me always to be sober, and I dropped other friendships which were based on long pub visits.

I joined the board of the local Citizens Advice Bureau (the national charity offering free and impartial advice to all), where Philip had been a trustee, and soon became vice-chair. I put my effort into running Camdata and resurrected my plans of building town houses in my garden.

The fog was clearing, and I was actually changing. I felt completely different from when I was a 'dry drunk', i.e. the period in 1995 when I was not drinking for five months after rehab in The Retreat in York. At that time, I hadn't actually stopped thinking like an alcoholic. I was just applying iron willpower, which will ultimately always fail, as inevitably a life event will come along where you can't resist turning to drink to cope. I had learned to admit that personal willpower is never enough. You need to admit you are powerless and need help before you can enter recovery properly. Now I was attending AA two or three times a week, I went to an AA convention in Dumfries and I was following the AA steps and mantras. I had much more time each waking day and was using that time beneficially.

Two years to the day of my first AA meeting, I decided to stop attending meetings. My AA friends were horrified, as members are generally expected to continue going, and many people keep this up – and absolutely need to keep it up – for the rest of their lives. I had given the 'main share', which is where a member talks for about thirty minutes about their own experiences and problems and aspirations, but because of holidays and rehearsals to do the lighting for Sheridan's *School for Scandal* I had been going to only about one AA meeting per month. I no longer belonged, partly as members' stories were becoming repetitive, but mostly as I felt I had moved on and created a new life. For AA, this is a very dangerous situation, as I was replacing my respect of and dependence on the AA group with self-control, which I had admitted eighteen months before at the Priory was not working for me. I was told I was always welcome back at an AA meeting whether I was still sober or had fallen off the wagon. However, I felt that I had made enough changes in my life and way of thinking and had enough in place to be able to 'fly solo'.

My recovery marked the end of what I call my 'lost decade', from the failure of Camdata in 1991 to entering recovery. I lived much more fully and achieved much more in the decades before and afterwards, both for others and myself. I've often felt that my drive after I stopped drinking was because I'd been much less efficient with my life during those ten 'lost' years. The bigger issue, at least for me, is that if I am actually genetically predisposed to addiction, have I redirected my addiction to something else? If that is the case – and I suspect it is – I believe that I am addicted to being busy, to experiences and to helping others. The point is that it is the obsessiveness that is providing the relief, not the alcohol itself. Being obsessively busy, always doing several things at once, and needing to feel over and over again that I have made a positive difference has replaced the alcoholism. If the alcohol had been an anaesthetic in the past, to dull the pain of personal loss and grief, this function is now fulfilled by my busy-ness. The worse the life event that befalls me, the quicker and more strongly I come into action: throwing myself into a practical response, hopefully one that is constructive and helpful to other people. I believe this is now one of my ways of anaesthetising myself.

Chapter 9
The AA Programme and Me

Without going into further detail about the AA programme, its steps and the many acronyms and mantras adopted by the AA community, here are some that have been meaningful to me. I describe them below in my own words.

One day at a time

This is one of the best-known AA mantras. The concept is that when you wake up, the 100% focus is to get through that day until you sleep again without picking up an alcoholic drink. You should not worry if you had a drink yesterday nor worry about picking up a drink tomorrow. With time, in my case, these days melded into a continuum, where I didn't need to think about not drinking every day. For me this took a few months, but I have met recovering alcoholics who need to concentrate on their sobriety for every remaining day of their lives.

In my view, 100% of alcoholics are mentally ill when practising alcoholism, which is both a physical and mental disease. I am of the opinion that addiction is an illness – this is not accepted by some of the medical profession, nor some of the general public. People who have no experience with or knowledge of addiction commonly think that not picking up a drink or stopping drinking before sleep takes over is 'just' a matter of self-control. I can emphatically say, that was not the case for me. I had tried self-control for several years, with zero success. Which is exactly what the first AA step says: 'We admitted we were powerless over alcohol – that our lives had become unmanageable'.

Plan, but do not project

My interpretation of this mantra is that a recovering alcoholic can plan things in the future, but must not project an outcome, as whether you succeed or fail may then become an excuse for a drink. Perhaps you are planning and hoping that a relationship with a child or spouse or parent will improve, but it is important not to project that will happen by a specific date or year or even ever.

Major changes should not be made until a recovering alcoholic has been sober for a year. The period of a year is arbitrary but in the case of many alcoholics, this is the time when the fuzz begins to clear, the days begin to settle into a new rhythm and, most importantly, behaviour changes become embedded.

People pleasing

People-pleasing behaviour can be dangerous in recovery from any addiction. It is important to take charge of your own life and not rely on others to make you feel good. The need to make others happy can become an excuse to relapse.

This one is difficult for me, as I have spent nearly fifty years in sales mode, whether working in the pub, in the electronics shop, building businesses or publishing books, including this one! They say that a well-negotiated sale is a win-win for the seller and the buyer, so I feel I am programmed to ensure that, in a business environment, my customers are 'pleased' with me, and this has leaked into my private life. Nonetheless, there is a compromise to be had between pleasing others and standing up for one's own rights and values and that's what I aim for now.

Progress not perfection

I learned at school, by trial and error, that homework, exam preparation and even exam performance is a trade-off between time spent (within one's capabilities) and the final outcome. Compromising the final quality of a piece of work is necessary if one is to avoid the pursuit of perfection soaking up too much time and effort.

This extended into my business life and possibly my private life. The AA meaning is that one should pursue personal growth using the AA principles rather than strive for perfection, similar to Buddhist principles. Having perfection as one's goal will almost always lead to disappointment and hence like any personal failure, an excuse for an alcoholic to pick up a drink. As a simple example, when I tiled my bathroom one time, I struggled to get the tiles (black ones, in true male fashion!) to be even in all three dimensions. Oh dear, let's have another neat gin.

Keep it simple, stupid (KISS)

Stress and over-complication can lead to temptation. This is another tough one for me. I tend to analyse probably more than I should, although having been an entrepreneur and then investor, risk analysis comes naturally to me. I can jump to quick decisions and although clearly not all are correct, I very rarely regret my decisions. At the other end of the spectrum I can procrastinate for months over something, forming lists of pros and cons. But whether one is overthinking is a very personal judgement. I have definitely missed opportunities because I have thought too long, both in business and personal situations, but I am also vulnerable to FOMO (Fear of Missing Out), which can lead to poorly thought-through decisions, with plenty of time for regret.

Sponsors

A sponsor is a senior member of AA or NA who has been in recovery for usually at least a year. A sponsor helps a newer

AA member to stay sober, to navigate membership, answer questions, work on the 12 steps, and offer accountability.

I'm sure that for me, having Mick as a sponsor made a big difference to my ongoing recovery. He drove me to AA meetings and supported me into meetings when I was scared of going.

And finally...

Why did I keep all the notes I had written and received from my time in the Priory over twenty-three years ago? I don't regard myself as a hoarder. I think it was that, if I felt like picking up a drink, I could remind myself of the really terrible times before my AA 'birthday' – the 23rd of March 2000. And nine years after that day, I was as close as I will ever be to using alcohol, when the police rang to say they had found a body and believed it was Ian's. But I didn't drink then, nor when Alan died in 2022, as will become clear later.

How have I remained sober? I have replaced alcoholic obsessiveness with other obsessiveness, giving myself too much to do, lots of varied experiences, activities and human connections. Of course there is also an element of self-control, there is habit, definitely fear of repeating the awful times, a sense of responsibility to my children, my partner, my friends and of course my own self-responsibility!

I have given back by spending five years as chair of Focus12, a local drug and alcohol rehabilitation charity supported by a number of national TV and music celebrities, helping other addicts to enter recovery. I had approached the founder and CEO, Chip, at an event and offered to help. I had been sober for six years and wanted to give back to other addicts, and my operational and strategic business experience was of use to them. I joined the trustee board and soon became chair. I have had many conversations with friends and colleagues about someone they know or love who they think drinks too much.

In fact, I have accidentally drunk alcohol: for instance, when a pub has served from the wrong bottle, or I have picked up the wrong pint of lager when playing pool or eaten desserts, like zabaglione, that contain alcohol and thus have felt a very slight euphoria. But this has never led me to voluntarily pick up a drink and it never will.

I have far too much to lose.

Chapter 10
Life in Recovery

I developed new ways of using my time, forged new friendships and thought through new ideas and opportunities. My driving licence ban still had eleven months to go, but I knew I would get it back in due course, and meanwhile Philip was very keen to chauffeur me whenever it suited both of us. I was very lucky to live in Stamford rather than a rural village, as it offered all the cultural, hospitality and shopping services that I needed, I had many friends there and it was well served by public transport.

Although recovery occurs 'one day at a time', I really believed that my sobriety might settle in for the long term, and I therefore had the confidence to commit to other roles. I decided that I ought to understand what it was like to be a board member of an organisation that I didn't own, something I had not done since I had been on committees at university over twenty years earlier. I wanted to learn how to do this, as I felt at some point I might be able to offer my skills and experience.

I joined the Stamford YMCA where I soon became vice-chair. As mentioned before, through Philip, I also joined the Stamford Citizens Advice Bureau (CAB), an organisation I would be involved with for over a decade. I learned a huge amount from the CAB, including how to merge two independent charities, and how to cope (or try to cope) with a board meeting that got so emotional that physical violence was threatened between two trustees. I tried twice to join the national CAB board, both times unsuccessfully. In addition, I helped rescue two CABs that were being shut down by their main funders, the local authorities.

I also decided that my relationship with Margaret would not work in the long term, as she didn't want to live together and I wanted to live as a couple, so we broke up and I tried something that had only recently been introduced in the UK: online dating. In early 2001 I met a number of women in my local area, as I had specified that I only wanted to meet people within a certain short distance from home. However, I met a woman called Alison through this online dating site, which matched us up although she actually lived fifty miles away, near Cambridge. Luckily, we met soon after my driving licence was returned, coincidentally on the same day that I received my one-year AA medal from the Priory in Nottingham, in March 2001. Seven days after we met, Alan and I flew to the USA on holiday, which meant that courting continued with expensive calls and the newly introduced text messaging.

My continuing sobriety meant that I could rebuild my relationship with the boys and my parents. I was reliable and they could talk to me and know that I would remember what was said. I was also able to have a good and steady relationship with Alison.

Alan had joined a football team in Cambridge and so we used to go down most weekends and stay with Alison and her three children. Alan and I settled into spending the working week in Stamford and weekends in Cambridge, and started to go on holiday with Alison and her kids. Alison and I wanted to make sure the relationship was strong and to let Alan finish his GCSEs before we moved in together, which meant that Alan could then take his A levels at a new school.

Ian had been living with me, but struggling at school, not because of a lack of academic ability, but through lack of focus and drive, and misuse of soft drugs. He left school after the first year of sixth form and travelled to Costa Rica and Ladakh in north-east India. He also worked in the UK before spending a year in New Zealand.

* * * * *

While I was still drinking, I had had another difficult episode with Camdata. Camdata had taken on a fixed price project which was beyond our capabilities and although we successfully delivered the required extra robust computers, we lost a lot of money, so I asked Gerry for help. He suggested we merge our businesses, as we had been working together for over ten years, so I would run Camdata as a division and he would provide all the back-office functions. Having worked for Gerry for a year, I bought the company back from him with the help of my supportive friend and supplier, Richard, and worked on growing the business, paying back Richard's loan in the process. About three years after this, after I got sober, Gerry decided he'd rather concentrate on building his free-range egg business and offered his technology company to me. It was an easy decision for me to buy it, and with the help of my engineer Pete I resurrected his company and that formed the core of Camdata for the following twenty years, making a thirty-times return on the purchase price.

I also set up a new business and called it Starfish Consultants, partly because of its alliteration with the word Stamford and partly because most starfish have five arms and I thought that as I diversified, I could be involved in a maximum of five roles at one time. As it turned out, I ended up with almost as many roles as a centipede has legs.

I had allowed the outline planning permission for four flats in my garden in Stamford to lapse, but I resurrected that plan in order to speculatively build three townhouses – probably the biggest financial risk I have taken in my life. The houses were half-built, I had borrowing from the bank and from Alison and had over £100,000 (in 2023 prices) of personal credit card debt, when the terrorist attack of 9/11 happened. The whole world was in turmoil, the USA was mourning thousands of deaths and preparing for war and no one knew whether and when there would be a huge geopolitical crisis and economic shock.

Fortunately, I managed to sell all three houses by the end of the following year. I then embarked on another property project, this time with my next-door neighbour in Stamford, called Julius, who owned a wine import business and had room in his car park for two houses, with a similar design to the three I had built.

Although working with Julius (who provided the working capital) showed how a partnership can be beneficial to both partners, we had more problems with this project than with my garden one. This was partly because the property market had cooled by the time the houses were ready to be sold and partly as I decided to use lead cladding as the front fascia. This needs zero maintenance compared with painted wood or render, but is not to everyone's taste. The biggest problem arose from a misunderstanding with Julius, which led to the piling company breaking both an electrical cable and a gas main when they started work, delaying the project by six months and causing consternation to many neighbours.

In spite of all of this, I had really caught the bug for property projects and went on to buy a 13th-century 2-star listed cottage from my barber, who was a friend, despite having to get permission from the Lincolnshire county archaeologist to develop it. This project entailed the most complex spiral staircase I have ever seen, a very slow sales process and a huge cost over-run, leading to a very large loss at the final reckoning. However, I am still very proud of the result and regard it as one of my legacies, despite the fact that only I recognise the efforts (and money) I expended on the property.

Next I bought two houses in Hull and refurbished them with the help of a local connection, Tim, whose company I enjoyed and who did good work when he was sober. I hope that, in the process, I contributed to his entry into recovery.

After Alison and I had been together for two years and while Alan was finishing his GCSEs, we sold my house in Stamford and I rented even nearer to Alan's school until Alison sold hers and we bought a house together. It was exciting to move into our new house in the village of Harston, just south of Cambridge and in the catchment area for her younger children's school. The house was quirky, being a large bungalow and at the end of a long linear village, where we didn't get to know many people. The villagers met mostly through the school, the church or the pubs, none of which we frequented. But we had a growing number of new friends through bridge, especially a couple called Sue and Pete, with whom we became particularly close. Alan had actually been bullied at school in Stamford, and the move to live with Alison and attend a local sixth form college significantly improved his outlook on life, although he rarely saw his mother, who lived fifty miles away and was overseas for at least half of the year. She had remarried, to a man she had first met thirty-five years earlier in Greenland, when they were both there on field trips. Martin was a gentle intelligent giant, who had been a policeman, then a dentist. He had retired early, owned half a hotel on the Island of Mull and was building a yacht.

In the first few months, I really missed Stamford and the friends I had made over the previous eight years. I found Cambridge too big and difficult to navigate, not in terms of the physical layout, but in terms of the people. In Stamford, I had been a reasonably large fish in a small pond and here I was a minnow in a lake. With hindsight, I realised I was still somewhat shy, and I felt my achievements so far were somewhat inferior to those of others. It is very easy to feel this in Cambridge, where there are Nobel prize winners round every corner and many people who are or have been global-level giants in their fields. The Cambridge business world is like a 'village' where one is accepted only once trust has been developed and one has helped others without charging for that advice.

In order to ease my way in, I joined a graduate society set up within the Computer Science department, where I had studied. This was run to help graduates with their careers rather than as an alumni fundraising project, and we had multiple events to connect the several thousand students who had studied in the department in the last thirty years or more. I set up a mentoring scheme and mentored a number of graduates myself, including someone who owned a water tower, which provided great views during our sessions! But it was working with another mentee, Martin Kleppmann, that was life-changing for me, as I invested in his startup, Ept Computing, then helped grow it and finally sell it. The process taught me many things about being a minority shareholder, being an external director, how to handle a co-founder leaving, pivoting and selling to a Cambridge software company. Martin went on to found his next company before completely handing over to the buyer, so we didn't get the full exit proceeds. I didn't invest in that one, which was a bit of a shame, since it became the first acquisition by LinkedIn after that company floated on NASDAQ. A good lesson there: don't worry about the ones that 'get away'. The really life-changing element of building and selling Ept Computing was that the exit allowed me to become a member of a group called Cambridge Angels in 2009. A business angel investor is someone who invests their own money in startup companies and often also helps guide them to success. Business angels commonly 'flock together', acting as a group and supporting each other and newbies on the scene, and the Cambridge Angels is such a group. More about this later.

This was also the peak of the time that I set up businesses, not all of which grew or even survived, from plans for a contract bridge clubhouse in Cambridge, to a number of separate technology companies, to two companies that undertook small and large property projects. I definitely made mistakes – none as expensive financially as the listed cottage, but many that proved financially unprofitable, although I learnt from each endeavour.

As it transpired, Starfish Consultants needed more than five arms, as I became the sales director of a medical technology company, set up an import business with a German manufacturer and bought up a competitor to Camdata.

One of my starfish arms was my role as part-time sales director of a local medical technology device that measured the wearer's ECG, movement, body temperature and respiratory rate. Designed initially to help identify injured soldiers' needs on a battlefield, I promoted it throughout Europe, which meant day trips to many cities throughout Europe to discuss its use with police, security guards and academic researchers. The device was also worn by the pilot of the first electric-only aircraft to fly around the world, the Swiss Solar Impulse. The medical technology company struggled to raise finance, partly because of the military connections, and I helped organise its sale.

Alison was a senior accountant and worked as a finance director or financial controller. She had the typical life of employees in Cambridge when working for a number of technology startups, which come and go and wax and wane in size: she was made redundant several times, but easily found another role every time. A colleague of mine, Andy Richards, coined the phrase 'Cambridge is a safe place to do risky things' and this applies to employment as well as entrepreneurs. Finding another role if your employment disappears is much easier than in other cities.

There was stability at home and the children all progressed through education and early work life. Times were good; we had sufficient income, although somewhat lumpy due to the property projects I was doing, we had good friends, holidays and hobbies, and I was remaining sober.

However, the calm was soon shattered. First, in 2001, a close university friend died hiking in Scotland, leaving behind his wife, Nancy, another close university friend, with young triplets and an older son. Although at the time I behaved reflexively to support her as best I could, some time later I began to feel the shock to me personally. He had been a close friend, I had known him very well, and it hit me hard.

In 2006, our family was shaken by a much closer death. I was sitting at my desk, when Christine's husband Martin rang to say that Christine had died suddenly at Johannesburg airport. She had been heading to South Africa for work, and it is thought that she had developed a DVT on that or previous flights, which had travelled around her body and caused a fatal pulmonary embolism. Martin said that he would ring Matt, but that I should contact Ian and Alan.

All three boys were in the UK at this time. Alan was at the start of his gap year and was working at a wine merchant in the next village, so I went to collect him, but Ian was working in Aberystwyth and I had to ring him.

Despite it having been a difficult separation and divorce a decade earlier, I experienced Christine's death as a great shock. I am still not sure how much of my grief was for my children who had lost their mum, or because of residual love I had for her. It was the definitive end of the life we had once thought to build together.

Christine was an only child and her father had died from a long illness just a few weeks earlier, so her elderly mother, Mary, was already grieving. Despite my bumpy relationship with Mary, I felt extremely sorry that she had lost her husband and then her only child. She was given a lift from Taunton to Peterborough for the cremation, which was attended by her, Martin and the three boys only. This was coincidentally Mary's 90th birthday and as it happens, she died a few weeks later. There is a medical term for a broken heart, first identified in Japan: takotsubo cardiomyopathy, where the left heart ventricle undergoes physical changes due to mental trauma or stress. I believe that was her fate.

Matt and Ian went to the Lake District to reflect and talk and after they came back, Christine's wake was held in Stamford.

Matt read the eulogy, and Alison and I attended, along with many friends. Ian found visiting Stamford very difficult, as it brought back many bad memories. While at school there, he had used soft drugs quite heavily. He had started having hallucinations around the town due to cannabis psychosis and would refuse to go to certain places. For me, it was an especially sad week, as a few days beforehand I had gone to the funeral of Wendy – our nanny Dawn's mum and my girlfriend of a dozen years before – who had died from stomach cancer.

Martin was in his sixties and had not been married before. He had a drink problem and had been banned twice for drink driving, but luckily he was sober when Christine died, just three years after they got married. He stayed sober for several years, making his yacht ready for the water, helped by Ian, and then solo sailing across the Atlantic to Trinidad, where he stopped to finish the yacht's interior.

Unfortunately, he started drinking again and despite Matt spending time with him in Trinidad and talking to local alcohol addiction services, he died from his addiction eleven years later in late 2017. Matt was the sole executor and main beneficiary, so moved back from Australia where he was working and living with his girlfriend at that time, via Martin's funeral in Trinidad, to live with us in Cambridge whilst he sold Martin's house in the Lake District.

Meanwhile, my sister Sue had settled into her own flat in Hull and I saw her every few months, combining this with seeing my parents and my tenants. She was occasionally working in charity shops, but her drinking was affecting her life. In the Christmas period of 2006, Alison and I had gone to Morocco (every other year, her children spent Christmas with their father), while Alan was staying with my parents, with whom he had closely bonded when they lived next door to us in the Old Dairy. The plan was that Sue, who lived a few miles away, would join them for Christmas Day. This wasn't to be. When my father and Alan went to collect her, she was slumped in the garden, drunk. They helped her back into her flat and left.

Matt was studying Design in London when his mother died, having switched from Marine Biology in Portsmouth. In London, he also worked in a trance music and cyber clothing shop in Camden Market. After her death he followed a friend to Verbier where he lived and worked for several years. Ian had travelled and worked abroad and in the UK before returning to the UK shortly before Christine's death. Alan had done well at school, and was in his gap year, working in Cambridge and South Africa, before going to Edinburgh University to study Sport and Recreational Management.

Their growing independence and the loss of their mum meant that the time we did spend together was even more important. For many years, I had been on holiday one-to-one with my boys. I had climbed Kilimanjaro with Matt and three other friends in 2002 and then Matt and I spent ten days in Borneo in 2007 climbing the highest point in south-east Asia, Mount Kinabalu. This was particularly noteworthy as we started in the dark in order to see the sunrise at the top, and overtook many other less experienced climbers along the path while we were on the world's highest cabled route, a cliff-edge path with a metal line fixed to the wall for safety. It was only on the way down that we saw that if we had fallen from that cliff, we would have dropped over a hundred metres. With Ian, I spent two weeks in South Africa, half on a self-drive safari in the Kruger National Park and half working our way down to Cape Town from Johannesburg, plus a week exploring the state of Texas. Alan and I had three trips to the USA, motoring and skiing, and later a week of scuba diving together on an island off Bali.

My parents had left the Stamford area in 2000, whilst I was at the Priory. They moved back to Market Weighton in Yorkshire and then four years later moved again, to the village of Cherry Burton, near Hull, where they had first lived after my dad's retirement. Dad kept busy with DIY and outdoor sports activities like hiking over muddy fields and Mum mostly stayed at home unless they were travelling. This they did frequently, particularly to the USA and to Australia, where my aunt and my brother David's widow lived. However, sixty years of smoking, too much drinking and a lack of exercise gradually caught up with my mother, and her health deteriorated.

Her last couple of years were painful to experience, partly because she was so frustrated by her diminishing quality of life and partly as I was supporting them from three hours' drive away.

This is the period when I worked out my view on the difference between healthspan and lifespan. My mother had about 100 weeks between the end of her good health (her healthspan) and her death (when her lifespan ended). So I would say her healthspan ended two years before she died. Of course this is just my personal view, but she did say several times that she was ready to die. My father, on the other hand, had only three weeks between independence and death.

My mother was diagnosed with breast cancer but refused treatment because her quality of life was poor – she had breathing problems, she was bedridden some of the time, could no longer travel and had lost some of her independence. The cancer metastasised, and it is probable that it had spread to her kidneys when she died. She had always said she did not want to go into a care home, as both my grandmothers had done, and she got her wish, although she did spend her last few weeks in an acute hospital in Hull. This was a rather grim place, which closed three months later. I remember the last time I saw my mum. I was walking down the corridor with my dad, who had been fifteen centimetres taller than me his whole life. As we walked, I realised he had shrunk with old age and sadness, right down to my height.

My mum died two weeks later and I am lucky that I have a positive memory of chatting to her during this last visit.

All the boys were in the UK and helped at her funeral, and that's the last photo I have of all three of them together.

After eighteen months at Edinburgh University, Alan came to me and said that he was not enjoying the academic work. In addition, he was having back problems that were so bad that he could no longer play rugby, which he had been doing at a high level. He and Matt planned to spend a ski season in the Canadian Rockies. I was disappointed about him dropping out of university but have always felt that I would be happy as long as my kids were happy and healthy. I am pretty convinced that going straight from school to university is not good for many kids, who need to mature and work out the meaning of life, particularly working for a while without a tertiary qualification, and then deciding whether they want to attend university in their early to mid-twenties.

So in the summer of 2009, all my boys were in the UK: Alan at home, working before he and Matt went to the USA later that year, and Ian living in Glastonbury.

After their mother died, her wealth went to her husband, Martin, but her parents' wealth bypassed her and was inherited by the three boys, once they reached the age of twenty-one. I had not been part of the writing of those wills, but I did hear that Christine wanted the age to be twenty-three, not twenty-one. Matt was already twenty-one, Ian would be turning twenty-one later that year, and Alan a couple of years later. After Christine's death, I was warned by an accountant friend that inheriting a fairly large sum at an early age can damage a person, and although I have no proof that happened, it certainly changed their outlook on life. Over the following years, the boys spent the money and although they worked long hours, they lived well beyond their income, enjoying themselves and seeing the world. Not what I had done, but who was I to expect them to follow my route in life, let alone attempt to force them down that path?

As mentioned before, I was chair of the Stamford CAB when I moved to the Cambridge area, and at the request of my local MP in Stamford and Grantham, Lord Quentin Davies, for continuity reasons I remained as treasurer to that office after finding a replacement chair. I also joined the Cambridge CAB soon after I moved to Cambridge in 2004, under chairman David Livesey, who had beaten me in an election for the main board of the National CAB. I am not sure anyone likes losing an election, but I respected David and worked with him for several years, partly as a trustee and then as an external contractor. I also became chair of the regional group of sixty-six CABs in East Anglia.

The Cambridge CAB was renting cramped offices and, with the help of a loan from a social investment bank, the charity wanted to buy better premises in order to offer many more interview rooms for clients and better working conditions for the staff and volunteers. I realised that I was able to offer an unusual combination of knowing the CAB service very well after more than a decade with them, while also having been closely involved in many property projects. I therefore stepped down from the board of the Cambridge CAB in 2008 so that I could project manage a building for them (the resignation was necessary, as generally, charity trustees cannot be paid for work associated with the charity). It was tough, but I am very proud of our achievement. I found a suitable building near Cambridge railway station, raised the funding, negotiated with the planners, the trustee board and the numerous contractors, all with the staunch assistance of the bureau's manager, Rachel.

The year 2009 started well. I had been accepted into the Cambridge Angels group, I was enjoying multiple charitable and commercial roles and was working to give Cambridge residents better access to their Citizens Advice Bureau. I was working on a technology project to help keep children safe at Butlins, which involved a fascinating work trip to India. I was playing plenty of bridge, skiing, attended a Cambridge May Ball for the first time in thirty-two years (this time as a security equipment supplier, not running a student disco as I had done in 1975!) and had become a freeman of the City of London. Then the most tragic event of my life so far happened.

Chapter 11

Ian

It was late July 2009 and I hadn't heard from Ian for a few weeks. We mostly communicated by text message, with occasional calls. As mentioned above, he'd been living in Glastonbury for the last couple of years, not working, but living off the inheritance from his maternal grandparents.

Glastonbury is an unusual town, attractive and in rolling English countryside, close to the location of the famous music festival. Many of the residents practise a New Age lifestyle, rejecting modern Western values, instead emphasising spiritual ideas and beliefs, astrology, alternative medicine, meditation and so on. There are many myths and legends related to the Glastonbury Tor, King Arthur and the confluence of ley lines. Ian was very spiritual and loved it in Glastonbury. He could mix with people who had similar values and views. He could relax and meditate. When he'd visited Ladakh, he'd lived with a local family and started to adopt some Buddhist principles. There he took the name Namgyal Essense, shortened to Nam, and this is how he was known in Glastonbury. Namgyal is a common Tibetan Buddhist name meaning 'victorious' and Essense may have been a reference to 'spirit'. As he was living from his inheritance, he had time to help others with their problems, whether those problems were emotional, spiritual or practical.

I had texted him several times, because I wanted to tell him about the annual reunion of Focus12, the drug and alcohol rehabilitation charity where I was chair of the trustees, and about my visit to my dad, his grandad, who was now alone after my mother died sixteen months earlier. But Ian hadn't replied. This was before the days of WhatsApp and it wasn't possible to see if a text had been received and if it had been read. I was becoming more and more uneasy, and had contacted one of his close friends, who told me Ian was in a better place than he'd been for a while.

On Tuesday the 11th of August 2009, I was working at my desk after having dinner with Alison, her children and Alan, who were now sitting in the lounge next door watching TV. I had done the annual appraisal of the Managing Director of a charity that I chaired and was emailing the trustees about the outcome when my mobile phone rang at 10.45pm.

I picked up the phone. The caller asked "Who's that?" I said, "Peter Cowley" and I immediately asked him the same question back. It was late at night and it was an unknown number. He said he was a police officer, giving his name, rank and police station. He was called Jarrod.

He went on to explain that the body of a young man had been washed up that day in a small cove along the coast near Bristol. A farmer had found him, and the body had been taken to a morgue, but although he was clothed and wearing a rucksack, his only possession was a ten-pound note. The body had some unusual tattoos and they had checked his fingerprints against a national database. The fingerprints appeared in the database under Ian's name and were linked to a mobile telephone number. That number was mine.

I said I didn't believe him and that I would ring his police station. Jarrod gave me the number, which I checked on the internet. I rang him back in total shock. He explained that Ian had been fingerprinted after an incident some time ago when he had been stopped for jumping over a London Underground barrier. Ian had given his real name, but my mobile number rather than his own.

It was necessary to confirm Ian's identity, but Jarrod said that it might not be possible for me to see his body, as he had been in the water for a while. But they could perhaps use the tattoos for identification. Ian had asked me to photograph his tattoos when I had last seen him four months before, so I emailed those through, and Jarrod confirmed my deepest fears.

I went into the living room where the others were still watching television and cried, "Ian is dead," collapsing onto the floor. We all hugged and cried together and I then rang Matt, who was not far away and who drove home immediately.

There was no way that I could sleep, so I stayed up all night and as our two very close friends Sue and Pete were both awake and recovering from elective transplant surgery, I went to see them at 4am for hugs and a coffee. Before I left the house, I sent an email to another friend:

I feel completely and utterly distraught.

The police rang late this evening and said they had found a body in the Severn and via a convoluted route had got my mobile number. They suspected it was Ian and his tattoos confirmed it.

I don't know what to say – what have I done wrong? Why haven't I been there for him when he needed me? – in the last few days and in the last few years and since he was born.

Not sure if it was suicide yet and won't know until I speak to the coroner in a few hours whether it is appropriate for me to see him.

Fuck Fuck Fuck

It was the third anniversary of Christine's death on Sunday and my only glimmer of positivity at the moment is that he strongly believed in an afterlife and if he is correct, he will now be with her.

Don't know much else. Alan was here and Matt came straight back from Northampton. Alison here.

But I'm stuck alone at this fucking computer crying my eyes out.

Overwhelmingly need to find out what happened – will go down to Bristol in next few days.

Need to work out what sort of funeral service (and/or celebratory wake) to have.

Will compose another round-robin death email – a sort of 3 year déjà vu.

Will need to have some help to avoid consuming myself with guilt. Matt is probably mature enough to get over it by himself, but Alan isn't.

Wonder if there is a note for us somewhere?

Then came the long and painful aftermath of his death. The police's first job was to determine if there had been foul play or not. While they were doing this, Ian's body could not be released for burial or cremation. However, the police were struggling with getting any friends or contacts of Ian's to help them. They asked me not to post anything on social media – this was 2009 and Facebook had entered the UK a short time before – but I got frustrated with their progress and decided to start doing my own investigation. I set up a Facebook memorial page, which soon led to someone coming forward to say they had seen Ian getting on a bus late the night before it was presumed he entered the water. However, this person was not willing to meet a police officer as there was a warrant out for his arrest. I arranged for him to give a statement in a solicitor's office, but eventually he went to a police station, without being arrested for his previous misdemeanour.

The CCTV from the bus had long been overwritten and the driver did not remember a very tall young man from several weeks before. The bus terminus was in a pretty seaside town on the Severn Estuary – a beautiful location with one of the largest tidal ranges in the world.

Ian had spent the day before in Bristol, and on one of my visits to the area trying to find out what had happened, a Glastonbury friend of his and I went to see some of the friends he'd spent time with there, meeting some people who were well outside of my comfort zone, as they were leading a very different lifestyle to mine. At one house, I was advised to wait in the car while Ian's friend went in. Within minutes of her return, she became extremely talkative and agitated. I had a flashback to the occasion seven years before, described in an earlier chapter, where I took two Priory friends to the funeral of a third and one of them had alcohol in her handbag, getting back in the car after a comfort break completely under the influence. The same thing seemed to have happened here. I never found out which drug Ian's friend had consumed, but our visit to Bristol was over and I drove her back to Glastonbury.

Illegal drugs were easy to obtain in Glastonbury and Ian no doubt used them, but I don't believe he was addicted to any substance, or that they played a role in his death.

Ian's laptop had disappeared and I found out who had taken it, so asked the police to get involved. Under pressure, the 'friend' of Ian returned it, inexpertly wiped. A Mac expert retrieved much of the hard disk but not enough to provide any more information.

There was no note, but there were some clues that he may have planned to take his own life. For instance, he had moved from a small rented house into a friend's spare room a few months earlier and had emptied his bank accounts by gifting cash to friends. Other incidents also now appeared in a different light, such as the fact that he had asked me to photograph his tattoos a few months before – although I can't now remember the reason he gave at the time – and that he ensured my mobile phone number was linked to his fingerprints through the incident of the Underground barrier. Once the inquest had been opened, which happened after the police decided there had been no foul play and passed the case on to the coroner, we were given an interim death certificate, and I used that to request access to his Hotmail account. I struggled with navigating Microsoft's bereavement process in the USA but luckily I knew someone senior in Microsoft and managed to sort that out, and they sent me a DVD of his emails. Unfortunately there were no answers within those emails.

Ian had sent a text to a close friend, who called himself Lucifer, which read:

Stand tall, shine brightly,
flow freely my brother
fly true

This was shown to me by Lucifer and had been sent at 5.33am on Tuesday the 4th of August (coincidentally what would have been my parents' 60th wedding anniversary). Many months after he died, his mobile phone company confirmed that this was sent via a mobile phone mast beside the Severn Bridge, which is within sight of the place where I believe he entered the water.

Meanwhile, Matt and Alan were booked to leave the UK in mid-September to travel and work in North America. It had been wonderful that they were around for the five weeks after Ian's death to share the grieving and help with tracking down his friends for the police. They also helped organise two celebrations of his life, one for Ian and one for Nam. The one for Ian was held on a nature reserve near Cambridge and was conducted by a humanist celebrant, who we knew through playing bridge in Cambridge. My father was there and many people came forward to describe their memories of Ian. The second was for Nam, and took place on a beautiful day in Glastonbury on the side of the Tor with everyone in colourful clothes. There was an Indian fire ceremony, where I, as his closest kin, sat cross-legged for two hours throwing ghee into the fire as the celebrant chanted. In the evening we set off many Chinese lanterns from the top of the Tor. Ian read and practised shamanism, and as I found after he died, he was loved and missed by so many people in Glastonbury.

Over a hundred people attended each event.

Eventually, foul play was ruled out, and Ian's body was released six weeks after Matt and Alan had finally flown to Los Angeles. It was really tough when they left Europe and I didn't see them again for several months. Alan didn't return to live in the UK for about three years and Matt for over twelve years.

Ian's body was cremated in early December, four months after his death. I collected his ashes soon after and also had the final meeting with the Detective Inspector in Weston-super-Mare. The inquest hearing was held nearly a year after his death. I had been to an inquest five years earlier to support a close university friend whose brother had taken his life in Cambridge. To prepare for Ian's hearing, I decided to attend another hearing in the coroner's court. The coroner's court is generally open to the public and anyone can attend, including the press. I knew no one there, and it felt inappropriate to be a witness to the proceedings where a family was angrily blaming the health service for their assumed lack of treatment, which in their view had led to the father's suicide. But it did help me get ready for Ian's inquest hearing, as it gave me a chance to familiarise myself with the court process.

By this time it was July 2010. Alison and I drove down to Bristol and as we were led into the courtroom, the court clerk took us to one side and told us it would be an open verdict. I had done some research and had already realised this was the most likely outcome. There was no evidence of foul play, no evidence of him taking his own life or of an accident, and there were no natural causes. It was not easy to sit through the hearing, which contained spoken witness statements from the police. For the death certificate I had been asked about Ian's occupation and I had put 'faith healer', which in the cold light of a court felt uncomfortable. As expected, an open verdict was given.

That evening we met nearly a hundred of his Glastonbury friends and spread a proportion of his ashes into the strong winds at the top of Glastonbury Tor. There were many group hugs and singing, as well as lots of laughter as the ashes were being blown back into our faces. We had a party in a local village hall, where the atmosphere was soon sweet from the many joints that were being rolled. This is of course normal for the Glastonbury culture – I had grown to love the people with whom Ian had spent his last two years.

After we had finally been able to lay him to rest, it took me at least another two years to develop my own narrative of how and why he died.

This was a process that I had never had to undertake before and it is only with hindsight that I realise what I did and how important it was for me.

In my view, at the start of 2009 Ian decided to take his life around the third anniversary of his mother's death. He had had a special bond with her which was reciprocated. As described previously, Christine had died on the 9th of August 2006, at the end of a flight to South Africa, from a pulmonary embolism, possibly caused by a DVT.

Understanding how someone can take their own life is very difficult. I knew that Ian's mental health had been affected by the misuse of potent cannabis in his late teens, but I believed that by him concentrating on his physical health and practising shamanism, he was living a clean, fulfilled life.

What helped me was to think that Ian had become Nam, and Nam believed he no longer needed his physical body, that his spirit would continue and perhaps that he would meet his mum again. I don't believe that Ian would have left his family and friends in such a distraught state, but Nam was a different being.

The narrative I created has meant I can think fondly of and miss Ian/Nam terribly, but not be consumed with grief and guilt. Guilt is a very common feeling of friends and family in cases of suicide. In my case, I felt guilty, of course, about the shortcomings in the boys' early upbringing. Even after I got sober, I felt that I hadn't done enough to offer emotional support, that I should have been closer to him, close enough to know what was going on with him. But with the help of the narrative I built up, I was able to work through these feelings and not let them destroy me.

In the period after his death, I learnt that there is such a thing as healthy guilt, where one recognises one has behaved inappropriately and should make amends and change one's behaviour. But that was not possible with Ian. I could not now make amends to him. Having said that, five years after his death I received an unusual email from someone who knew him who is a practising medium. He said he had heard from Ian and asked if I wanted to make contact. I didn't reply, although am now becoming tempted to do so.

Ian had given most of his possessions away, leaving his poetry, a few books, clothes and a ten-pound note. On the 3rd of August, he went to Bristol to see friends – although there were no reports of him saying goodbye – and then caught the last bus to the place where he entered the water.

He probably spent the night there, meditating and preparing himself, waiting until daylight, when the tide was highest. Then he sent his last text to his friend and entered the water. I am unbelievably thankful that his body was washed up a week later, otherwise, he would still be missing and how could I cope with that?

At the start of this chapter, I described how one of his close friends, whom I contacted when I hadn't heard from him, had said Ian was 'in a better place', i.e. feeling better than he had been for a while. I have since found out that in cases of suicide, this can be a result of a momentous decision having been made.

*   *   *   *   *

Grieving and trying to cope was so hard. In the first instance, during and after the police phone call, I immediately went into denial and that continued for several months. The coroner did not want me to see his body after it had been in the sea for a week. I knew I could have pushed, and in fact two people offered to travel to Bristol with me and go in first and make the decision for me, whether it would be a positive or negative. It would not have been my first time seeing a dead body – I had seen my brother's and mother's bodies in the funeral homes – but on the other hand, if the image is very upsetting one can never unsee it. The two people were my close friend Alan Dunckley and a media personality I had met who had also lost a son to suicide at a similar age to Ian, and who had been public about the loss.

I thanked them both, but decided that my last memory of Ian should be the weekend we had together in Cambridge in April, when we had been playing badminton. At two games all and 13 to 13 points, he had slipped and twisted his ankle – a draw. Had Ian deliberately created this outcome? The ankle was damaged enough to visit our local A&E and there we bumped into a close friend of his from his school fifty miles away, who was a nurse. Another coincidence? Once X-rayed and bandaged, we went to the cinema.

That weekend, Ian had asked me to photograph all his tattoos. I don't remember what reason he gave, and I didn't think anything of it at the time, but it meant that I didn't have to identify his body a few months later in the morgue. Although I will never be able to prove it, I believe he planned it like that.

Another part of grieving is anger. My anger was fairly short-lived and centred on the lack of a note. Over time I read all his poetry and other writings, all his emails and what was left of his hard disk. I could understand why he would not tell anyone he was going to end his life, in case someone talked him out of it, or prevented him by physically intervening (although that would have been temporary), but I like answers, and a note may have given them, even if he had directed any anger and frustration at me.

He had an older laptop, which was with his clothes in the rented room, and on it was a note:

Ian Cowley Dead

I had imagined that there should be another line that said:

Namgyal Essense Lives On

I misinterpreted the note for too long, until I realised it meant that the laptop belonged to him and that it had irrevocably stopped working.

I had been seeing a business coach called Caroline before Ian died, to work out what to do with my charity board positions, as I had ambitions of joining the board of a national charity. Caroline was also a counsellor (my higher power intervening?), so I moved from sitting opposite her to being on the couch with her with a box of tissues between us. I was very lucky that I had that working relationship. It meant I could visit within a couple of days after the police phone call and she really helped me. I also visited the annual conference of an organisation called SOBS (Survivors of Bereavement by Suicide), where the most memorable talk was from a train driver. One thinks of family and friends, and perhaps the emergency services, being affected by suicide, but I had not thought of the 5% of UK suicides involving trains and the awful experience this entails for the drivers of those trains.

One of my coping mechanisms whilst grieving for Ian, you won't by now be surprised to learn, was definitely keeping busy and trying not to let people down. When he died, I was busy with the CAB building project and many other things. Helping the police investigate Ian's death took precedence, as did organising memorial events for him in Cambridge and Glastonbury together with Matt and Alan. In order to get away from England for a while, Alison and I and two friends went to Naples and the Amalfi coast.

But I think my grieving was having an effect on my physical health – I had a number of minor ailments that took me to the doctor a few times, with no conclusion, before they gradually faded. Perhaps they were psychosomatic, perhaps not. But then I had an event that really worried me. Sitting at my desk, a spot of flickering triangles appeared in both eyes, that gradually grew so it became an arc that covered much of my vision. It faded away after fifteen minutes, but not before I had googled it and rung my GP. My internet research agreed with the GP's telephone suggestion of a TIA or mini-stroke. This led to a worrying weekend, although it didn't happen again and I had no other symptoms. The GP referred me for a carotid MRI, and the result was reassuring – not a TIA but a scintillating scotoma. This is a visual aura that can precede a migraine, although an associated headache did not happen in my case.

We didn't travel far that Christmas, spending just a few nights in the Cotswolds. I remember being grief-stricken at midnight on New Year's Eve and wandering around in the snow outside a hotel whilst others celebrated the start of 2010 with 'Auld Lang Syne'.

Alison and friends such as Sue and Pete and Nancy (the university friend who had lost her husband a few years previously) provided a great deal of support, but I am sure I busied myself even more than before, just for distraction.

Many years later I had a number of sessions with another therapist, trying to answer the question of whether I had processed Ian's death enough, so that, should I become senile or develop dementia with old age, the grief would not resurface in a way that I wouldn't be able to handle. I can't remember how this thought was triggered in me, but I was really worried about it. It was good to shed tears whilst I went through his death again with someone new, but we didn't reach a conclusion.

The mind works in mysterious ways, and it is only in the last couple of years that I have been able to bring to mind the name of the place where he entered the water, without having to look it up, when discussing Ian's death. I spent over a decade describing it as a town between Bristol and Weston-super-Mare.

I have been back to the town and the cove where his body was found a handful of times, and back to Glastonbury on many occasions.

I started spreading Ian's ashes in 2010, and fourteen years later his ashes have been spread in about 120 locations around the world, mostly in the sea which he loved and where he died. There is a map on his memorial website with pins in all the locations, with at least one in many of the ninety or so countries I have visited in the world. I would very often do the spreading with family or friends and it has become a kind of pilgrimage. Like his siblings, he loved to travel, and I like to think that, despite his death aged just twenty-three, he has continued travelling in the afterlife. Carrying bags of grey-white powder in luggage has occasionally triggered an airport check.

Chapter 12

Public Success

"And the United Kingdom Business Angel of the Year 2014 is… Peter Cowley!"

Five years after Ian's death, I was in the neo-Gothic Liverpool Cathedral, completed in the 1970s and the largest religious building in the UK, seated at one of many beautifully decorated and atmospherically lit dining tables. We were all there for the annual awards ceremony of the UK Business Angel Association, the trade body for angel investing, run by its co-founder Jenny Tooth. 'Angel of the Year' was the last of about a dozen awards. Just a few minutes earlier, photos of the eight entrants had been displayed on a large screen and I had started to feel quite nervous. Then, incredibly, my name was announced as the winner and I went up to the stage to receive the beautiful glass award and say the few words that I had scribbled down, just in case I might need them. It was unbelievably special to be so honoured by the UK trade body in front of a community of 300, and especially in that location: to be crowned 'Angel of the Year' in a religious building, as an agnostic, is quite something.

You may remember that my business angel career started through investing in Ept Computing back in 2007. In the building and selling of that company with Martin I cut my teeth as an angel investor and the exit led to me becoming a member of the Cambridge Angels.

However, before I was introduced to the Cambridge Angels, I made another angel investment. I had met an interesting person, called Ian, on a government funded project, and he invited me to join him in founding a company, Eluceda, which invented a very quick (a few minutes) method of detecting MRSA, primarily a hospital-acquired infection, resistant to a number of widely used antibiotics. This is a real issue in the UK, as elsewhere in the world. I was on the board for a few years.

In the autumn of 2009, the year we lost Ian, I went to my first Cambridge Angels pitch event as a guest. This is where entrepreneurs give presentations to potential investors. Two important events happened that evening. I met a bright and friendly guy called Paul Anson. It was the first Cambridge Angel event for both of us, although he was a more experienced angel investor than me. I had only made the two angel investments at this point. Secondly, I met three entrepreneurs with whom I have been on a thirteen-year journey as a shareholder and investor director in their company called Plumis, which provides fire suppression systems for private homes.

Both Paul and I were accepted into the club. Besides more informal meetings, the CA also hold dinners for members, and one day, at one of these dinners, I sat next to another member, Robert Marshall, the fourth generation of a Cambridge-based family business called Marshall of Cambridge (Holdings) Ltd, founded in 1909, which then had several thousand employees in aerospace engineering and car distribution, as well as owning and operating Cambridge Airport.

Robert mentioned that he was looking for a bright young person to help the company invest in early-stage technology companies. I said I was definitely not young and no one can identify themselves as bright, but I was definitely interested. He was an engineer, like me, and we both wanted to help early-stage companies, me with time and a little bit of money, he and his company with connections and a lot more money.

A couple of Thai meals later, I met the Marshall CFO, Bill, and also Robert's father, Sir Michael Marshall, chairman of Marshall at the time. I got to know Sir Michael well over the next eight years and came to think of him as much a gentleman as my own father.

And hence, with the agreement of the Marshall board, Martlet was founded. This name was chosen because the mythical bird of that name is on the crest of Pembroke, the Cambridge College where both Bill and Robert had studied, but I like the fact that in heraldry, it is a bird that has no legs and hence is always on the wing learning from and observing the world below.

This was a turning point for me, as it meant I would spend one or two days per week sourcing investment deals and helping startups grow. It also meant that my relatively small investment was leveraged by the Martlet money. Our philosophy was to be part of an angel round (in those days called a seed round, and now commonly known as a pre-seed round) writing one of the bigger 'cheques'. The investment committee consisted of three engineers (Sir Michael, Robert and me) plus an accountant (Bill) so, like all early-stage investors, we tended to invest in technology that we understood, especially hardware (rather than software) which frightens most angels, for good reason. Software companies scale by increasing the computing power, but hardware requires long design cycles, component sourcing, stocking and physical distribution, all of which limit the rate of building a business, so they are not so attractive to angel investors, since more capital is required and the risk of failure is higher.

We were going to launch on the 1st of April 2011, but decided to avoid any April Fool's jokes by delaying until Monday the 4th. Looking back, although I had access to huge and easily accessible experience in investing from the Cambridge Angels, it took me a year or two to learn that one should invest in people and not plans. The abilities, experience, mindset and coachability of founders are so much more important than any plan that they have written, although of course a plan is necessary to justify how and where the investment money will be used.

Around this time, I led an angel investment round into a startup called Arachnys, which provided extended due diligence to financial institutions. This is one of my success stories in terms of the help I could provide to the founder, David, what I learnt from him and the company's growth, and the eventual sale of the company a decade later.

Alison and I invested in ten new startups in 2011 alone, partly as I wanted to ensure that Martlet built up a portfolio (Alison and I always co-invested with them with our own money) and partly because I was like a kid in a sweet shop, getting too excited by passionate entrepreneurs with interesting ideas. But one has to learn somehow, and twelve years later, six of those have gone bust, two still exist and two have been sold. However, I have made several times more money on the two exits than the total I lost on the failures; angel investing is a numbers game with a dose of luck.

One of the failures was eGo aeroplanes. These planes were a cool Apple-esque product, loved by all aviators and wannabe fliers – pure white with an iPad as a control panel. I joined the board, where I both contributed and learned, but although many potential buyers said they'd love one, few actually bought one. This was mainly due to over-engineering, which pushed up the price. Unfortunately, the company folded a few years later, having sold just two aircraft.

Two years later, I invested in and joined the board of another startup that eventually failed, called Captive Media. Gordon, its CEO, had been on *Dragons' Den*, where he'd been resoundingly told that all the dragons were 'out'. But we, a group of Angels, decided we were 'in', and put in over two million pounds over the next few years. Gordon had come up with a novel and imaginative way of advertising to the notoriously difficult target group of eighteen-to-thirty-five-year-old males. The company strap line was 'the world's first contact-free, networked, interactive washroom media system […] with hands-free control', and it was based on men in urinals aiming their stream to control the animation of a skier or beer bottle moving around the screen just above the urinal. The company built hundreds of installations in the male toilets of pubs and gave hundreds of thousands of hours of amusement, but the advertising revenue was not quite at a level to keep investors believing in Gordon's dream long enough for the company to become profitable, so sadly, it folded. However, I regarded that journey as an 'elegant failure', as Captive Media shut down without owing a penny to anyone except the investors.

Another interesting company I invested in and joined the board of was a startup that was building a robot to pick strawberries, which, following David Cameron's Brexit vote debacle, has a lot of potential, as most UK strawberries used to be picked by workers from Eastern Europe.

Besides my angel investment activities, I continued working for charities in this period, and during the summer of 2010 the CAB building was completed and ready for occupation. The CAB chair, David, knew Lord Mervyn King, the governor of the Bank of England at that time, who agreed to open the building. This generated good local press coverage. I had the honour of showing Mervyn around the building, and was told not to mention the economy (this was in the middle of a global financial crisis) but to talk about his interests – cricket and Aston Villa, about both of which I knew almost nothing. It all worked out, because he is skilled at talking to all sorts of people. I simply concentrated on telling him about the building and the charity.

As my angel investing activities expanded, so did my experience and network. In 2014 I successfully applied for a role as a member of the Investment Committee of the Angel CoFund (ACF), and I was appointed. The ACF is a £100 million fund set up with UK taxpayers' money to co-invest with angel investors in startups. I had applied a couple of times for ACF co-investment myself and thus had been on the other side of the table. It had been many years since I had been interviewed for a role, and although I thought it would not make much difference to my life whether I got the role or not, I was proven wrong a few months after joining the organisation.

Unbeknownst to me, the person who runs the Angel CoFund, called Tim Mills, had entered me as the UK Business Angel Association (UKBAA) Angel of the Year award. A week or two before the event, the Managing Director, Jenny, had rung me suggesting I attend the annual conference. I had attended previous UKBAA events in London, but this was in Liverpool, and I needed to be in Birmingham at 9am the morning after the award dinner, so I wasn't keen. To convince me, Jenny suggested I ring the previous year's winner, close friend and angel investor, Rajat, so I did and he said it was probably a good idea to travel to Liverpool, not just to learn from the event but in case I won.

After the photographs and congratulations, I walked back to my car and drove two hours to a hotel in the Midlands. What was so important that I needed to drive through the late night was the chance to test-drive the first hybrid Audi in the UK, which I had pre-ordered. I'd driven diesel cars for many years due to the better fuel consumption and running costs. Some years I'd driven over 35,000 miles. But being on the board of a company called Vantage Power, who were converting London double decker buses into hybrid vehicles, had taught me a lot about the dangers of diesel emissions and hence I knew I had to swap to petrol, or even better, hybrid. The Tesla S had not been introduced into the UK yet and the hybrid Audi was an excellent car.

Of course, there is no such thing as a 'free lunch' and so the UKBAA award came with a commitment to help UKBAA at events, lecturing, judging and on panels, and, although I was only five years into my angel investing journey, I had learned enough to be able to help educate others.

As a direct result of the award, my public profile increased exponentially. This soon became something I needed to address. I was discovering that as one becomes more well-known in one's field, an increasing number of people will ask for one's help or advice (and money!).

With incredible serendipity – my higher power intervening? – a month before the award, I had met an entrepreneur called Katy Tuncer at a networking dinner in Cambridge. Although we didn't speak that evening, Katy decided she'd ask my advice about her startup. We met and she explained that her company Ready Steady Mums, an outdoors exercise class for new mothers, was not doing well. Katy had been a business coach for many years starting at McKinsey, and Ready Steady Mums was a side gig. Now she wanted help to work out what was wrong, which I said I'd gladly do. As she left, she thanked me and then told me that I had a problem with saying no. She had observed that I had said I'd help her, but was actually so busy that I should not be taking on anything new. We agreed that I'd help her with her company and, in return, she would coach me.

And so we started helping each other and became close friends. The ultimate demise of her startup is described in *The Invested Investor*, my book about angel investing, as another example of an 'elegant failure'; the company closed solvently, losing money only for the investors (most of whom said they would invest in her next business) and the 'failure' actually continued for many years as a successful project within a charity. In return, Katy worked on my working life, initially helping reduce my twenty-three(!) roles to seventeen (still proving the starfish analogy incorrect) and then helping me identify what I wanted from my business life, which had a positive effect on the time available for my personal life. Katy helped me with my brand, my priorities and my goals (which I never completely worked out). In turn, I helped Katy set up and grow her company, Horizon37, an IP-rich leadership development business, which grew from retained profits and hence chose not to take external investment.

In 2015, my public profile increased even further, as a friend, Chris Smith, invited me to provide a five-minute technology slot every month or so on his long-established radio programme called *The Naked Scientists*, broadcast live on BBC local radio and later on BBC Radio 5 and in other countries, and as a podcast. The programme had a total audience of several hundred thousand each week.

The week's producer and I would decide on a current topic: AI, social media, security, food technology and so on, and then I would prepare to answer a few questions. Chris had a habit of chipping in with a left-field question and this gave me great experience in thinking rapidly and answering to the limit of my knowledge and opinion without fabricating, whilst on live radio. The most amusing incident was a live 'outside broadcast' in the BBC Cambridge studio car park about drones. I bought a cheap drone and tried to learn how to fly it in our garden, hampered by the trees. On the night, we went outside, the drone took off under my control, flew and then I made a mistake and crashed it, causing the words "Oh shit" to escape me. Chris winced and then I said, "Fuck, I swore." This was all broadcast live to many thousands of listeners in East Anglia. In accordance with BBC protocol, Chris took over, apologised a few times while trying to sound sincere and not corpse live on air. And we rerecorded the clip for non-live audiences, when Chris (a couple of decades younger than me) took over the controller and flew it perfectly, despite this being his first time controlling a drone. The controller is identical to computer game controllers, but I had grown up before the advent of such games.

Meanwhile, Camdata was still going. I had another attempt at growing it by taking on a part-time sales director. He tried his best, but the markets where we had had success in the 80s, 90s, and 00s were gone and I didn't want to allocate enough time and money to pivot the business, so it continued as a lifestyle business.

A while later, I decided it was time to reorganise the company. I classed it as a lifestyle business but that was not strictly true, as, although it was interesting to run, I hadn't taken any money out for several years and in fact had kept it afloat with loans, which had reached nearly £100,000. A particularly bad experience with a supplier triggered a rethink, which I worked through with Katy. Camdata had been putting together a system for a provider of waterless toilets for sub-Saharan Africa and UK music festivals, which was both interesting, profitable and had a social outcome. We delivered it on time and within budget, but the effort behind the scenes by my engineer and me was painful, having to cope with a sub-contractor who had a minor breakdown at a key moment.

I decided to cease custom hardware and software projects, to stop the development and manufacture of all products and to concentrate on importing, distributing and repairing the products for the traffic light industry.

This meant that Pete, who had joined me twenty-six years earlier and had been through thick and thin with me, including the business failure, my alcoholism, the company sale and repurchase, would need to be redeployed. I offered to give him the custom business, which he didn't want, so I made him redundant (in his late fifties) but facilitated a job at one of my investee companies, where he stayed for a few years before retiring.

This meant putting in new processes and software systems, unwinding from a few customers (many of whom bought spares) and setting up a repair workshop at home. Soon after, I rolled up my sleeves, heated up a soldering iron and started the repairs myself, which I really enjoyed. It was like being a geeky teenager again.

My £100,000 director's loan was repaid within a few years and Camdata finally became a real lifestyle business: that is to say, a business set up and run primarily with the aim of providing a living or maintaining a certain lifestyle. At the same time, Martlet was growing as we found more and more investment opportunities. My investment activity together with Alison had continued and we now had nearly fifty separate investments, some of which had gone bust, but others had actually exited for a profit on our investment.

I had set up my own angel investing website, where I listed my investments, successes, failures (with reasons for their demise) and statistics. (I have been told several times by people that I am the most transparent angel they have ever met.) My seventeen investment rules are also to be found on the site, and one of them is not to invest in founders straight out of university. However, on one occasion, I made an exception to this rule. Raph and Gideon had met at Cambridge University, and joined probably the best startup accelerator in the UK (Entrepreneur First). I liked what they had decided to do: combining electronics and building construction with technology that measured the temperature of concrete (which emits heat as it sets) and hence increasing the speed of construction, as one can build onto the concrete slab much sooner than the standard method, which requires concrete samples to be sent miles away to a laboratory. Both Raph and Gideon are excellent learners and, boy, did they have a lot to learn! I stayed on the board for three years whilst we raised funding, tried to get the product working and built a customer base.

In 2016 I had my first major exit. I was on the board of a university spin-out (that is, a company founded as a result of a research project where the researchers and the university believe they can commercialise the Intellectual Property generated by that project – the company is then said to have 'spun out' of the university). This particular spin-out was a materials science company which had developed and manufactured a very low cost and tiny gas sensor, and we sold the business to a large

Austrian company. I am somewhat embarrassed to say that I then swapped my 70mpg (4 litres/100km) hybrid Audi for a bright red Porsche! Not very practical as my main car as it was the 'poor man's Porsche', a Cayman S, which has no rear seats. I have lost count of how many 'mid-life crisis cars' I have owned, even without being in a mid-life crisis.

Back in Cambridge, alongside continuing to chair Focus12, the drug and alcohol charity, I was asked to join the board of a school, the Cambridge Centre for Sixth Form Studies, which had been set up thirty years before and converted to charity status. I soon became chair, which meant that on the charities front, I had now been involved with advice, healthcare and educational charities. One of the biggest lessons from this role was the difference between running an agile startup that can change its offering within weeks or months and a school that has to plan two or three years ahead with educational and extracurricular programmes. I was lucky to work with an excellent head, Stuart, who had an engineering degree and an MBA in addition to many years' experience as a teacher. We worked well together on the challenges of ensuring we had enough students joining each year and providing them with a good education.

In 2015, we planned the sale of the operational business of the school to an entrepreneur. This would have resulted in a trust with at least £10 million to distribute to educational causes in the UK and the global south, and would have produced a much greater charitable outcome than continuing to operate the school. I stepped off the board to help the school's trustee board and headteacher get a good deal with the entrepreneur and his private equity backer. But the deal failed and a few years later the charity was handed over at no cost to another Cambridge private school. I very rarely feel regret, but the erosion of this £10 million is one of my bigger disappointments. I had a vision and a method to achieve that, and it failed.

Meanwhile, I had joined the board of UKBAA, and during that period got to know about the European Business Angel Network (EBAN) which became an important part of my life especially when I became their President. I attended their annual conference in Zagreb, Croatia and was on stage soon after Bruce Dickinson of Iron Maiden fame, who is now a motivational speaker. At the dinner that evening, I was encouraged by my friend Brian, an Iron Maiden fan in his youth, to ask for an autograph for the one and only time in my life, from a willing but rather surprised Bruce Dickinson.

As I took on more numerous and higher-profile roles, my brand was growing. I loved what I was doing, helping entrepreneurs, and found that I didn't need to market myself so much anymore. Every year, I received over 1500 investment pitch decks, where startup entrepreneurs apply for investment funding, of which I would invest in six or seven after weeding through them with the help of my mentee, Tom. Tom was a friend of one of Alison's children and had knocked on my door one day, saying he wanted to get into investment management, so I took him under my wing, mentored him and gave him experience in all parts of my business life.

At the EBAN conference in Zagreb, I had met a Turkish entrepreneur who invited me to his angel investing event in Istanbul, which led to me joining his board and being awarded a trophy, which was amusingly entitled 'Peter Cowley – Angel of the World', but without a year. Was this a forever award? Or had someone forgotten to engrave the date? I still have the piece of glass, but have received much more meaningful awards both before and since.

As I continued on my journey as a business angel, I started to consider more and more what I could do to educate a new generation, to share my experience and spread the word. So I started to become involved in other types of activities. For instance, my close friend Richard Lucas and I set up Camentrepreneurs.

Richard is an expert on setting up community groups throughout the world, and we had a vision, mostly driven by Richard, that we could help anyone who had graduated from Cambridge, or other universities, by enabling events throughout the world for entrepreneurs to meet, connect and learn from each other.

In 2016 I became chair of the Cambridge Angels, something I had unsuccessfully tried to do three years earlier. I had learnt a lot from the friend, John, who had beaten me in that vote, so was now ready to take over the role. The organisation was fifteen years old and I immediately set about researching whether it was still fit for purpose and whether we should make any changes. The whole board was behind this idea and as a board we worked through a number of projects and strategy sessions, with Katy's help. The result was a decision to propose to the membership to take on more paid help, increasing the small team's resources by a factor of four, which of course meant increasing the membership fees (Cambridge Angels has never taken fees from the companies in which it invests – the organisation is fully funded by members). This turned into one of the most tense AGMs I have ever chaired. Although the proposal was adopted, several people voted against, including one of my board, and it was followed by several resignations, although in all cases, these people were replaced by more active members. I remember having a scintillating scotoma (the condition which caused my eyesight to be dominated by flashing triangles first experienced after Ian's death) whilst on stage – surely triggered by the stress.

I was still thinking about how to make a bigger impact in helping angels and entrepreneurs, resulting in projects such as Camentrepreneurs. I'd investigated ideas of running an entrepreneurial event in Cambridge or setting up a new society, such as a livery company, which would be based in Cambridge rather than London.

That year, I had spent a week in Tel Aviv speaking to entrepreneurs, investors and technology transfer offices and was very impressed with the activity there. I wanted to help put Cambridge more on the map as a place to be entrepreneurial. The city has a history of being too modest in promoting its abilities to generate Intellectual Property and building businesses, in my and many others' views. I was invited a couple of times to visit the UK government Treasury to discuss how policy could help increase entrepreneurial success.

Personally, I wanted to help more people beyond mentoring entrepreneurs one-to-one or lecturing to thirty people at a time. I worked out that I had spent over 50,000 hours working as an entrepreneur and over 15,000 hours as an angel investor, so decided to start a podcast series and possibly write a book.

As will be explained later, when we pick up the story of our private lives once more, Alan was based in Cambridge at that time, starting his part-time master's degree. He was working in a pub as a shift manager, but he needed more income, so I suggested he and I founded our own startup. An inspired idea by my friend Brian resulted in us calling our startup The Invested Investor. Alan and I owned it 50/50, and he ran it with some help from me. I would fund it until it got to breakeven. Alan built a team around him of marketing and events specialists, a podcast editor and advisors and we published our first podcast in September 2017. He learnt how to do the accounts, how to run a social media campaign, how to manage staff and contractors, how to build a website and how to build a community and, in time, how to source printing and cope with the complexities of being a seller on Amazon. The last of those, after long conversations with helplines, led to Alan emailing Jeff Bezos and getting a rapid and helpful reply, although of course not from the CEO himself.

We found a local author, Kate Kirk, to help write the first book, called *The Invested Investor*, and then built a team to help with the marketing of the book.

Producing the book was a fascinating journey. Alan organised and recorded over eighty podcasts and ran a small promotional team using social media and events. I was interviewed for over thirty hours by Kate, who wrote the book based on those interviews. Together with many volunteer readers and editors, the book took about 500 hours from concept to printer. We contracted a *Private Eye* cartoonist, Neil Kerber, to produce twenty cartoons using his distinctive style. I particularly like the back cover image, which shows my rather irreverent habit of wearing shorts, even to formal events in Cambridge colleges.

Alan and I held the book launch in October 2018 with around 200 guests. I was really pleased to find that we sold 500 within a few weeks of the launch and in time, over 3,000 in total. But of course, the purpose of the book wasn't to make money (as most books don't anyway, even through a publisher), nor to build my own brand; it was to educate others and hopefully make an impact.

Somehow I got busier still. They say that if you want something done, ask a busy person, but I definitely took on too much. I was on nine startup boards, although sometimes as an 'observer', which is less of a commitment. I was still chair of the Cambridge Angels, although this became much less time-consuming once we hired what is called a 'deal sourcer', by name of Emmi. I accidentally called her our 'Deal Sorcerer' – a job title that amused her and which she immediately adopted.

I had been approached by the current President of the European Business Angel Network (EBAN), Candace Johnson, whilst giving a talk in Dubai just before Christmas, to ask if I would take over the role of President. This I pondered for several months, talking it through with Katy and others. Candace said I was the only person she could think of who might be able to remerge the two European angel investment trade bodies, which had split in a difficult way several years earlier. A friend who knew the situation much better than me told me the offer was somewhat of a poisoned chalice, and with hindsight, she made a good point.

I decided to go for it and in Sofia, Bulgaria, that June, I was elected to the board and immediately to the presidency. I have chaired many organisations but only after having been on the board for a while, getting to know the board members, values and processes. In this case, it was straight into the deep end, with a board of twenty-six members who hailed from Finland to Portugal and Ireland to Russia. Over the next two-and-a-half years, I learnt more about the varied mentality of our European friends than I had in the previous four decades put together.

As you might expect from someone who loves numbers and data, I have kept all my sent emails since the year 2000, and in my busiest years I sent over 13,000 emails and I guess received well over 100,000 each year. My working hours (although I still didn't feel it was work, as I enjoyed 95% of what I did) were becoming ridiculous. My need to keep busy and to feel I was contributing and helping people all the time meant I could no longer keep on top of everything. I was letting people down, not getting enough sleep, and it didn't help my relationship either. I talked to Katy, and she asked me to produce some data. My spreadsheet shows that my by now 27 roles were averaging 62 hours per week, 52 weeks per year (which if I allowed for 30 days holiday per year, equated to 70-hour working weeks). We produced a plan to reduce that to 48 hours per week, 52 weeks per year: still a ridiculously high number!

The Invested Investor was a success in terms of helping others. Besides the sale of a total of 4,500 printed books, ebooks and audiobooks, the podcasts had had at least 10,000 listeners. However, we still couldn't work out a sustainable strategy, so a friend and coach, Ludo, helped us work out a plan. Unfortunately, the ideas that transpired were to run events and training, which didn't suit either Alan or me.

Alan then decided he wanted more security, career prospects and to be part of a bigger team, which all come from being employed. He thought about becoming a teacher, an operations director or a venture capitalist, all of which I fully supported. After some soul searching, he became an investment analyst in Martlet. Apart from the introduction, I had no part in the recruitment process, and so I moved from being managed by Alan as CEO of The Invested Investor to working alongside him. He continued to run the now much less active The Invested Investor and Camdata. Camdata was three years older than him, and he had taken it over from me a few years before.

We launched our second book in December 2019, entitled *Founder to Founder*, which was mostly the work of Alan and Kate. This was based on asking the hundred or so people that we had interviewed for our podcast what advice they would give to a founder at an earlier stage of being an entrepreneur.

I had also started to look ahead to the next decades of my life. I had for some years intended to stop investing in new startups on my 65th birthday. It generally takes ten to twelve years from company formation to achieve a good exit, if it doesn't fail, which usually happens in a shorter timespan. I wanted almost all my angel portfolio to be 'finished' by the time I reached my late seventies.

I was still fully involved in growing the Martlet venture capital portfolio and also invested in and joined the board of a company, Spotta, that can detect bed bugs. And finally after ten years of investing, I began to see more of my portfolio companies being sold, hence returning some of the cash I had invested. I was on the board of two of these, including Vantage Power, which had reached the point at which so many of my failures have to give up their dreams.

Vantage Power had a really great team, excellent innovative technology, and some trial buses driving around London, but we couldn't convince our customers to commit to buying the hybrid engines in volume. And the founders, Alex and Toby, could not convince the current investors nor new ones to continue supporting the company.

I needed to have a frank talk with Alex about how the company was progressing, and after a fun afternoon together, we had a very difficult conversation about the cost of running the company compared with the availability of shareholder cash. Alex took this to heart in a positive way and reduced the company costs by nearly half, and they started doing paid engineering development work for customers, to bring in income.

For a few months it was really touch and go, and we had an insolvency practitioner joining the board at every meeting to assure us that we should continue trading.

The customer income led to good working relationships and when we decided to sell the company, the corporate broker already had several potential acquirers to approach. But what would they pay for a company that was failing?

This is when Alex 'pulled a rabbit out of a hat', as I like to refer to it, and sold the company for a sum that gave a good return for the founders and all the early investors, even though it would have failed within a few weeks, as the UK tax authorities were delaying paying a Research and Development tax credit. Basically, the acquirer bought the company for the team and the intellectual property: what is called an 'acquihire'.

As the icing on the cake, Alex and Toby managed to ensure the investors were paid more than the expected earn-out. An earn-out consists of future payments after the company has been sold, based on targets for sales or profitability, or, as in Vantage Power's case, keeping the team together for a further three years.

In 2013 I had invested in and joined the board of a company that had developed software to manage a warehouse, similar to the fulfilment part of Amazon. The software was being tested on a tiny 'warehouse' with a few racks of shelves and a few customers. Both founders were called James, hence they chose James and James Fulfilment as their company name. Over the following six years, we grew the business to over 100 employees and profitable sales of over £15 million per year.

By 2018, we had decided to bring a strategic investor into the company and because we were significantly profitable, we could raise money from a Private Equity firm. I could then sell my shares and the two founders could sell some of theirs. Venture Capital companies generally don't like existing investors to 'cash out', i.e. withdraw their investment, when they, the VCs, invest. This is because the VCs want all the cash they invest to be used to grow the company even faster. Private Equity investors, however, are comfortable with some money being taken out by founders and investors.

The James and James exit was progressing well, and on the 5th of March 2020, which was the date of the first confirmed Covid death in the UK and eighteen days before the first lockdown in the UK, I experienced my second company exit event where I was a board member. The first was when we had sold Ept Computing to Redgate Software in Cambridge (a database tools development company). Martin and I signed a lot of documents with the founders of Redgate in their solicitor's offices and then we all had a cup of tea to celebrate.

But the James and James exit was completely different. We got to our solicitor's offices in London at lunchtime and did not get back home until 4am. By this time, people were starting to expect a UK lockdown and the atmosphere was beginning to change. There was fear in the air, events were starting to be cancelled and we wondered if the private equity house, LDC (Lloyds Development Capital), would change their minds.

To my surprise, there were still points to be discussed, so there were lots of cups of tea whilst trying to avoid discussing Covid until our solicitor, Inger Anson, decided we should move to the buyer's solicitors. It was now mid-evening and the atmosphere was quite jolly. The people required for the meeting were arriving, and it looked like they were coming from home or a night out, and pizza and beer arrived. This was a different world to the one I was used to and I was quite uncomfortable with the joviality. People were a bit drunk and there was lots of laughter, whereas to me it was a serious occasion. We were trying to close the biggest deal I'd ever been involved with, there were huge sums of money (by our standards) involved, and it might have all gone wrong. It all felt inappropriate.

The senior management of LDC had actually spent most of the day working out how to support companies in their portfolio that would be affected by Covid, such as hospitality and travel. However, we thought we'd be safe as, if the UK locked down like many countries were planning, online shopping and therefore fulfilment would increase.

Eventually, all the documents had been signed except the final one from LDC. By this time, it was 2am and their CEO was not contactable. This led to another slightly tense period for us, until the signature followed in the morning and the money arrived a few days later. I had bought 4% of James and James in 2013 and six-and-a-half years later I had sold my shares for 107 times what I paid for them. I wasn't allowed to invest much as the company didn't need the money and the founders didn't want to sell much of the company, but the result was, if not exactly life-changing, at least 'house-changing' for both Alison and me (by this time, we had separated, as will be discussed in a later chapter, but we still held a number of joint investments together). This exit paid back all the money we had invested as business angels to date; the 'breakeven' point for angels, where it is only upwards from there. I have since found that many angels never reach that point, and if they do it often takes ten years. It took eleven years for me.

The year 2020 was memorable for the whole world, and tragic for many individuals, including one of my Spanish EBAN board members, who lost three close relatives to Covid within a week. Like many active angels, during the Covid year I had put more money into several of my startup companies to keep them alive whilst the situation was so uncertain. Some companies really struggled as they had no access to the university laboratories, or staff adjusted to working from home, or customer negotiation became more difficult. However, some thrived, including a company I had invested in several years before that made high-quality face masks. Previously, the main use had been in polluted cities and suddenly the pandemic increased its revenue tenfold. But for how long?

Whilst President of EBAN I had been working on merging the two European trade bodies, and that proved much more difficult over Zoom. We needed to rebuild trust and mutual respect and I believe that is done much more efficiently in the same room and over dinner. EBAN has a wonderful full-time director Jacopo (from whom incidentally I learnt much about how to cook steak to perfection), so the core business soon adapted to online operation. As chair, I was in charge of the board and helping to design and implement strategy.

Disappointingly, at the end of the year, the merger failed. I took that quite hard. I had put a lot of time and even more emotional effort into the process, and in AA-speak you could say that I had 'projected a positive outcome'.

I decided not to stand for a second two-year term and a very capable angel investor from Finland, called Janne Jormalainen, took over the role. All EBAN chairs become President Emeritus, which proved useful for opening doors, and meant that I could still be involved with EBAN as much or as little as I liked.

Chapter 13
Losing Dad and Sue

Whilst I was building up my angel investing career, family life did not stand still either, even if life would never be the same again with Ian gone. Going back in time about a decade, and picking up the story of our private lives, Matt and Alan, after arriving in North America mid-September 2009, had bought a large SUV in Los Angeles. They then drove this to Banff in Canada the long way round, via Florida, adding 6,000 miles and masses of great adventures, many of which I have not been told about, but definitely involving police encounters, plenty of couch-surfing, some deep-sea fishing and sky diving, and meeting many interesting people.

They then started working as ski instructors in Banff, renting an apartment, which I visited in March to catch up with them. I also skied, albeit at a fraction of their ability, and together with them spread some of Ian's ashes for the first time.

My father was coping with his new life. Following my mother's death, he no longer had a caring role, and possibly the only positive from her long illness was that he had learnt to cook and clean and do the washing, tasks that my mother had done for the previous sixty years. He also increased his circle of friends, who enjoyed his positive outlook on life. He kept as active as he could with outdoor activities and gardening and travel, including a cruise to visit Türkiye and Egypt and a trip to Australia to see David's widow, Susie, as well as my aunt and cousins and, importantly, to spread some of my mother's ashes at Emily Gap near Alice Springs, a location she loved.

Soon after the IBM Personal Computer became affordable in the early 90s, I gave him one and he soon learnt DOS and how to use a word processor. Several years after Windows was introduced, I upgraded the computer, so he could connect to the internet, although he always refused to enter his credit card details. After my mother died, his support calls to me when Windows 'misbehaved' became more frequent, and I began to notice his mental acuity had changed, although he was still fiercely independent. My mother had refused to touch a computer keyboard and I was very proud of how my dad embraced new technology, well after he had retired.

As well as Türkiye and Egypt, my father also wanted to visit India and Russia, all places that hadn't interested my mother. He never made it to India, but Alison and I had a few days in Moscow with him, shortly after Ian's inquest. This was tough for all of us and especially Dad, as Moscow was suffering its highest-ever temperatures of over 100°F (38°C), which had caused forest fires around the city. However, we visited the Kremlin and the wonderful underground metro system, and although Dad was understandably slow, we were patient and travelled at his pace. He was happy to have ticked off another place on his bucket list. Shortly after we returned he went up in a glider for the first time since his RAF training during the war, and the photo of him wearing a parachute and beaming wildly is one of the best memories I have. Since Mum had died, I travelled up to see him in Hull more frequently, often combining this with visiting the company Eluceda in York, or my sister, cousins and friends in Hull.

Alison and I had had a week in Israel with friends travelling around the country where I celebrated my 55th birthday and spread some of Ian's ashes in the Dead Sea, only to return home to a call from my father, in a state of distress that I had never experienced before. He'd had three minor car accidents over the previous few days, so I drove up to spend time with him. I found him to be physically well, albeit a little less steady on his feet, but very distressed about his car accidents. He could not understand what had happened, had not driven since then, and I had the very difficult conversation which many of us have to have with their elderly parents about stopping driving. This hit him very hard. He had loved driving – it represented his independence and he believed his social life relied on his car.

We got an emergency appointment and went to see his GP that evening, who suggested some tests. I felt really angry with the GP's response, as I didn't think he showed enough concern and didn't outline a clear route forward. I wanted him to do something. However, I forgave him a week later, when we found out how little my dad had shared with anyone about his health. I took his car keys and hid them in his house, which was very painful for both of us, and we went out to dinner with a very close friend of his, Margaret, who had been a nurse, a matron and then part of the management in a local hospital.

I drove back to Cambridge and Margaret, who was widowed and lived in the next village, said she would see Dad at least once a day. Two days later she rang from his house to say that he'd fallen and she couldn't lift him. She suggested she should ring 999, to which I immediately agreed. Two-and-a-half years earlier, my father had done the same with my mother. She'd been refusing to have contact with medics, but then had a fall. My father could have lifted her, but calling the ambulance was an excuse to get the health system to check her over. Margaret and I now plotted to do the same with Dad. The ambulance duly came and Dad was taken to hospital. Margaret went with him, and as she told me later, he proposed to her in the ambulance, to which she replied that she was greatly honoured and would accept him!

My sister lived a bus ride from his hospital and visited him before I went up to Hull three days later. An MRI scan had been taken, which found evidence of a stroke several months earlier, and evidence of two very recent strokes, which they said could explain the car accidents. Although he had many visitors, he was unhappy and wanted to leave. It was in the hospital that I found to my astonishment that he had dentures and no teeth, which he said had been taken out decades earlier, as was quite common in those days – and he'd been a dentist his whole working life!

It was clear that he needed help at home, and my sister and I found a care home five minutes' walk from her flat, which had a room, even if it was only for a few weeks or months.

However, a week later, I had a call from the consultant advising me to visit urgently as there was news. Alison and I rushed up to Hull, over two hours' drive away, to find that the consultant was just about to go to a funeral, but luckily he agreed to see us. He told us that new scans had found bowel cancer that had spread. I am sure that Dad had known something was wrong, but didn't want to be treated. For reasons I never quite understood, both his mental and physical health suddenly deteriorated very fast.

My sister and I then looked for a hospice and found a place. However, on the day before the manager went to assess him in hospital, Dad had tried to get out of bed and fallen, breaking his femur, which meant they couldn't take him.

The hospital made the same comment as they had about my mum – that he would last about a week. In both of their cases, they died exactly a week later, both on a Friday afternoon. Alan, who had flown back from New Zealand where he had been working after the Rockies ski season in Banff, went to see Dad together with me, and we started to think about what to do with his house if he was going into the hospice. The last time we saw Dad, he had stopped being able to speak, but recognised us. He died a few hours later, shortly before my sister arrived to see him, much to her sadness.

Although this period was traumatic for Dad, Alan, my sister and me, I am so grateful that it was only three weeks between him losing his independence and his death.

Some weeks before, Dad and I had booked a flight to Cornwall to have some time together and to spread my mother's ashes in the sea in St Ives (a summer holiday destination from her childhood in the 1930s), which would have given me a chance to talk to him about where he wanted his ashes scattered. That had been due to happen three days after he went into hospital, so I never had the chance to have that conversation.

It was so good to have Alan back home to provide physical and emotional support with the funeral and sorting Dad's house out before we rented it out for a few years. Matt couldn't make it back to the UK for the funeral, as he and Alan had gone to Central America after the ski season, and he had broken his jaw while in Mexico. He was stuck in the USA having treatment.

I was very worried about my sister being drunk at the funeral, but she came good and helped. Dad had appreciated the humanist celebrant at Ian's Cambridge funeral and so we found one for his funeral, with the exit music being one of his favourite tunes, 'The Dam Busters March'.

Although all three of my children were at my mum's funeral, only Alan was at my dad's, and a few weeks later, Alan and I were hiking the Milford Track (supposedly 'the best walk in the world') in New Zealand. Alison joined us and, with Alan, we celebrated Christmas in Auckland with his ex-nanny, now our friend, Dawn and her husband Giles, taking a trip to Waiheke Island to spread some of Ian's ashes at the vineyard where he had worked. Matt couldn't join us for this either, as by this time, he had repatriated to the UK for the NHS to repair his jaw. When it was time for us to go home, we first celebrated New Year in Auckland and then again in Hawaii, having flown for eight hours and lost a day. A cool thing to do, but exhausting!

Matt had his jaw fixed and lived at home with Alison and me for almost a year, helping sort my parents' house, working locally and helping with several of my business interests. He was twenty-six and although we were sad when he headed back to the Alps in December to work in Zermatt, it cannot have been easy for him living at home, after having been abroad for six years. Matt loves the mountains, and Cambridge is probably one of the flattest areas of the UK.

He and I had an adventure that year when we climbed the highest mountain in Norway, called Galdhøppigen. It looked tough on paper: 1,300 metres of ascent and about 7km distance each way, but it was even worse in real life. The walk up was on soft snow, so with each step we took, we sank many centimetres into the snow. Luckily, this was made slightly easier by following a group of teenage schoolkids, which turned out to be very useful, as we were in cloud for most of the route and left to our own devices might have struggled to find the top! After we got to the top, where predictably we couldn't see beyond a few metres, we had to get down again. This we achieved by walking, sometimes sinking into the snow up to our waists, and by sliding on plastic sheets where we could.

At Easter of 2012, Matt did something which caused me the most worry about any of my boys in my whole life. He and two friends bought a rickshaw in southern India for the Adventurists Rickshaw Run. Summarised on their website as follows:

> *Here's all the information you need to round up a couple of mates and drive a 3-wheeled shit box across the length and breadth of India. Over 3,000 kilometres of ridiculousness awaits you...*

This in itself was worrying. The rickshaw broke down literally dozens of times and although it was repairable by a mechanic wherever they were, that took time, and although it was not a race, they had to get to the end by a certain date. So they broke two cardinal rules: no driving on highways and no driving at night. If you've ever been to India, you will know that heavy vehicles drive at speed at night with no lights and on both sides of the road, and that if a rickshaw hits a bullock, the bullock wins. I was terrified.

Matt texted his location to a website, but only when he had a mobile signal and remembered to do so. There were periods of days when I lost contact, and I had intense memories of when Ian had died three years beforehand, after no contact for a few weeks. However, Matt finished it without mishap, Alan then joined him and they ski-mountaineered in northern India, before Matt visited his stepfather in Trinidad and returned to Zermatt for another winter season of ski instructing.

Alan returned to Australia and joined a gold exploration company, spending four weeks in the outback, working ninety-plus hours a week, then having two weeks off. He was the most junior member of the crew of four who were drilling holes and taking samples. It was a no-alcohol camp and so they had to be creative in their entertainment. He told us of the time that the four men took turns to read *Fifty Shades of Grey* out loud to each other, the famously raunchy bestseller of that year.

Meanwhile, I had been with a group of investors and academics helping entrepreneurs in China and I met Alan on an island off Bali, where he learnt to scuba dive. I'd been diving, although not often, since I was a teenager. Alan seemed to learn well during the training sessions in a pool, but both the instructor and I forgot to tell him one vital fact.

We went out together with the instructor and swam with fish and a giant turtle, but we went a bit deeper than the PADI-recommended twelve metres for beginners, and he hadn't been told to equalise the pressure in his mask as we descended. This is done the same way as one does on an aeroplane, that is, by holding your nose and swallowing. The result of Alan failing to do this was not painful to him, but it was unsightly, as he broke many blood vessels in his eyes. The whites of his eyes were red for days afterwards. But it was a great week together. We had simultaneous massages, talked a lot about life and unsteadily rode bicycles on unlit sandy tracks in the dark.

However, many years on the rugby pitch, followed by a skiing accident in the Himalayas and then kneeling for weeks on end removing soil samples from the drilling bit in Australia led to knee issues for Alan, so he decided to return home for an operation. Once he was back home, he decided to stay. He had been travelling for three years and to be honest, I envied him for the experiences he'd had and the people he'd met.

In 2013, my younger sister Sue's health deteriorated. She had returned from the USA and moved into a flat in Hull about a dozen years earlier, and had settled into a life of which I knew little. I had visited Hull less frequently after my father died, but we were in touch by text and occasional telephone call, although neither of us was particularly good at chatting on the phone simply to catch up.

Once I'd gone up with Alan to see her and also the tenants of the three houses I still owned near her. We went to her flat, which was fairly large with a lovely outlook over a Victorian park in central Hull, and found it untidy and dirty. The numerous animals she kept seemed healthy and Sue was sober, as she was every time I visited her because she always had at least a day's notice, but she didn't seem to feel the need to clean the flat. I wasn't sure whether this was because we were siblings or because of an underlying issue with her lifestyle. Alan thought the latter and got quite angry with me for not intervening. I had taken her to some AA meetings when she got back to Hull, but she wasn't ready to stop drinking. I know from my own experience, and that of many others through the charity I had chaired, that intervention rarely works. The addicted person needs to reach their own rock bottom. I wondered if Alan was right, if I should try to get her into rehab. But what was the meaning of 'get' in that sentence? Strongly encourage? Force? Physically bundle into a car and drop at the gates? So I did nothing.

Alison and I were spending a weekend in Milan over my 58th birthday, facilitated by a short-lived attempt by a small airline to fly from Cambridge Airport to various European destinations. At mid-morning on the Sunday, I had a phone call from Sue, saying she was in hospital and that she wanted to see us very urgently. We found a return flight as quickly as possible and back in the UK, rushed home to collect Alan, who was still living with us, and drove up to Hull.

She'd collapsed at home and had been taken to hospital, where she had been for a few days by the time we got there. She was stable, not unhappy, poorly but chatty. She wanted us to record all her internet and banking passwords and feed her animals, which we did. It wasn't clear what was wrong with her, and it was late on a Sunday so no one at the hospital could (or would?) tell us.

We stayed at a local hotel and did our best at her flat, which was much more of a mess than before, and we arranged for a neighbour to feed the animals. However, she had also asked us to rehome them. The three of us speculated – was she expecting to move in with Alison and me? Was she expecting to enter a care home, at the age of fifty-one with no savings and not much income? Or was she expecting the worst?

We contacted an animal rescue centre that took the animals and went home later that day. I went up to Hull again a few days later for a proper discussion, as Sue was much perkier and had been moved to a bed further away from the nurses' room. However, to my dismay, she described a procedure where she had had rubber bands tied to vessels in her throat to stop the blood leaking.

Some months before, she had been in hospital to have liquid drained from her abdomen and, although I knew about this, I had not questioned her explanation at the time. Sue now explained that it had built up again and the technical term for the condition is ascites, which in her case was due to cirrhosis of the liver. Despite my own alcoholism and chairmanship of the addiction charity, I had never heard of this and once again realised how little I knew about the human body.

Sue explained that she had been told that she needed a new liver, but that she would not be considered for a transplant until she had been sober for six months. We talked about where she should live once she left hospital and I explained that she could stay with Alison and me for a short time, but if she drank, we would find her a flat local to us (which we would have done anyway as soon as we could). I asked the nurses when they expected her to be ready to be released, as she was so much better than the previous weekend. I got a gentle but non-committal reply.

Subsequent events showed that she knew more from the doctors than she had told me. I went home, planning to go back to Hull the following weekend. She had a few local friends visit her during the week and I was told that she had been moved close to the nurses' station again due to deterioration. On Sunday the 13th of October 2013 I caught an early train up to Hull and found a very different person. She was clearly in pain and had been dosed with tramadol, an opioid pain medication drug she knew from her days as a groom, as it has veterinary usages. I don't know what dose she had been given, but she was very amusing in a somewhat incoherent way. I took a video to show her later. I still thought there was going to be a 'later' for her, then. She was now in a single room.

Close friends of mine in Hull, called Ruth and Mike, agreed to meet me just outside the hospital for a coffee and moral support. Whilst we were there, the hospital rang and suggested I return urgently. I did and her room was full of medics. She was still conscious and in a lot of pain. I knew that she had told the doctors not to resuscitate her, but I was immediately and rapidly ushered out again into a nearby waiting room.

About fifteen minutes later, one of the doctors came into the waiting room and told me it was all over. She had died. I was invited back into her room and given time on my own with her. She was composed with a smile on her face, with her eyes shut. She looked at peace.

I spent a while saying goodbye. On the way out, I asked a nurse (it was late on a Sunday evening) what had happened and was introduced to the most senior person on duty. I knew I'd been kept in the dark when I had asked on previous visits, but hadn't at those times wanted to take up their valuable time by pushing for more information. This time I was more determined to find out exactly what had been going on. I was told that from their experience with people on the renal ward with ascites, they had expected a significant and rapid deterioration – they just didn't know when. There was a massive infection going on in her body and her body was too weak to fight it, even with large doses of antibiotics. In such circumstances, death is almost inevitable.

I felt so sorry for her, for my children who had lost an aunt, but I was relieved that my parents had not had another child pre-decease them.

Alan drove up that evening to join me in Hull. He had been living at home with us working at the local examination syndicate and in a pub, before starting a degree at Anglia Ruskin University, the other university in Cambridge, where he graduated. We spent the next day working through the various tasks that need to be undertaken upon a death. He was a great help, both practically and emotionally.

My sister had specifically asked not to have people attend her funeral, so we organised a cremation a few days later at 8:30am. However, after speaking to some of her friends, I decided to organise a memorial event. Alan helped me with obtaining her death certificate, visiting the bank and the other practicalities. The most difficult problem was her flat, but it turned out that she knew her landlord very well and had even given him a debit card, so he could withdraw the rent from her bank account, taking trust to another level. Alan and I met him, liked him and he kindly agreed to clear the flat, donating or recycling the furniture and other contents, after we had taken everything that we thought we as a family might want to keep, such as her medals for attending the Barcelona and Los Angeles Olympic Games as a groom to a medal winner.

Again, I was reminded of the depths to which a person can sink due to alcoholism. Sue was far too proud to ask to be given or lent money and in the weeks preceding her death she had pawned our mother's jewellery. Fortunately, I managed to track down and buy back some of it. Within the paperwork in her flat were her medical records and they made for difficult reading. There were so many things she hadn't told me about – she'd had many medical interventions and had been much more ill than I'd been told. It was difficult to feel that I hadn't been 'allowed' to support her. But she was a grown woman when she died and had absolutely no obligation to share her ill health with me.

By speaking to her neighbours in the block of flats, I built my own narrative around why her health deteriorated so rapidly. She had a cat, which had died a few weeks earlier, and I was told that her drinking had increased after the cat's death, possibly due to a feeling of guilt, or to the loss of her closest companion. When we met in hospital, there was a sense that she had given up with life, which I recognised from the last stages of my own drinking.

Sue may have decided that life was no longer worth living with her addiction, but I believe she was clearly in denial and didn't recognise the connection between stopping drinking and life improvements. That was despite seeing the vast improvements to my life as I settled into sobriety. She once said that she would stop drinking once she got to the age that I was when I stopped. She was six-and-a-half years younger than me, and that time came and went without her doing anything to stop, as did a further seven years before she finally died.

I have often reflected on what more I could and perhaps should have done – forcing an intervention on her by taking her to rehab? Taking her to more AA meetings? Helping her move down to Cambridge to spend more time with her? In the end, she was an intelligent adult and had responsibility for her own health and life.

My boys were twenty-nine and twenty-five when Sue died. She had been abroad when they were young, so they rarely saw each other, and by the time she returned to Hull, they were progressing their education and then travelling. As their mum was an only child and my brother died before they were born, she was their only aunt and they had no uncles. I'd been very close to one of my uncles and to one of my aunts, and really valued those relationships, so felt sorry that they were missing out on that. My other concern was that my sons now had only me as a direct blood relation – their brother, their mother, all their grandparents and their only aunt had now died and they had no cousins. Although my relationship with my twelve cousins has been intermittent and varied in closeness, I still regard all of them as family. My boys never had that.

We held Sue's memorial event a few weeks later in the Midlands, so that her friends from the showjumping community could drive there from Cheshire, Yorkshire and Nottinghamshire. Some came from London, and others flew in from Europe and the USA. Her closest friend, David, who she knew from the USA, lived near New York and came over for the event.

At the memorial, people shared their stories both formally and informally – most were extremely funny – and it was clear that Sue was loved by many, as is shown particularly by the following story, told by close friend and colleague Helen:

"I wasn't meant to be a showjumping groom. I had no idea what I was doing, and for some reason Sue decided to protect me and my charges from myself. My first international show was in Holland, and thank goodness we doubled up on our lorry with Sue and Geoff's horses. All was well until we reached the docks at Harwich, where I discovered one of our younger and more excitable horses had nosed open the feed locker and eaten most of a bag of oats. Sue counselled me to keep my mouth shut, and we both hoped that the horse wouldn't explode with my rider on top. He never found out why most of the grooms and riders followed him down to the exercise ring that first day – he thought they were admiring his new horse. They weren't. Sue had started a book on whether he'd survive the warm-up. He did, and to this day he remains oblivious. I also discovered on that trip that I get really, really seasick. Half an hour into an eight-hour crossing and I was sheet-white and unable to function. Sue, despite never having met me before, packed me off to bed and looked after my horses until we got to the Hook of Holland. She hunted down some travel pills for the return journey too. She nannied me throughout the show, making sure I understood the perks and pitfalls, where to go and when to do things. Another memory is from Graz, Austria. Sue knew her horses so well, I saw her take Rodeo down to the collecting ring for some exercise. She mounted up, sat on him for two strides, jumped off and went for a lunge rein. Rodeo lived up to his name, bucking and leaping everywhere. "I should have left him for Geoff," she laughed. I have other stories, which involve copious amounts of alcohol, me getting drunk and Sue covering for me. Once she came to find me as I was late getting down to the collecting ring. I was sitting on the floor next to my horse, giggling hysterically and trying to put an overreach boot on without picking the hoof up. She sorted my horse out, propped me up, and made me stand by the ropes holding various horses for grooms while they helped my rider warm up, so he wouldn't find out quite how drunk I really was. Different people will have different memories and different versions of her, but to me, she was my idol and my saviour. I adored her, and she treated me like a slightly irritating little sister who had to be saved from her own mistakes. Back then we didn't have mobile phones or social media, and when I left the showjumping world we lost touch. I never forgot her, and I will always be thankful to her. I was deeply upset when I heard she had passed on. I hope she's rioting up there with Rodeo and the others, and partying like only she could."

Some stories were quite sad. Her drinking was, at times, out of hand, even whilst she was working.

I brought Sue's ashes with us to the memorial, but kept them in an urn under the food table. Her friend David is a very sensitive soul and I'd been told that he would have found it difficult to be confronted by the urn.

Sorting her estate was very simple since she had no assets and very little debt.

As for myself, my main feeling was one of relief, because her life in recent years had been terrible. For me, the grieving had started to happen years before. Due to her condition, we had not been able to have the sibling relationship I would have liked, and it had been hard supporting her while she continued in denial of her addiction. I'd lost a brother already and had been hoping to be close to her as a sister. I saw the relationship of my father and his two brothers and would have liked to have had that. I lost much of that when my brother David died and the remainder when Sue died.

Chapter 14
Calm Waters

The years following Sue's death saw a fairly steady family life, although they started with a number of health issues.

In 2013, Matt had a snowboarding accident in Zermatt, where, although he continued as an instructor for several months, he damaged his ankle. He spent most of the rest of the year in Geneva, visiting a clinic to have the problem investigated and then operated on in a much more major way, where both bone and its blood supply were rerouted from his leg into his rebuilt ankle.

As mentioned, Alan had had an operation on his knee after his return from the Australian outback. It now appeared that this didn't recover as quickly as expected, and from that, his alert GP suspected then tested for a condition called ankylosing spondylitis. This is an auto-immune disease, like rheumatism, which mainly affects the spine and if untreated, causes the vertebrae to fuse, turning one's back into a solid rod. It commonly starts in young adults. Although there are now good treatments, it causes pain. With the use of a gradually increasing intensity of medication Alan continued to live life as before: skiing, hiking and playing squash, although if he forgot to renew his medication, he ended up in bed for one or two days, due to the pain.

I was starting to experience more health problems, too. First, I began to notice a strange heart issue, an unusual beat a few times a day, so I had this diagnosed as an ectopic heartbeat. This is where the heart beats too soon and can't complete a full cycle. It feels like a heartbeat has been missed. I found this quite disturbing, but after wearing a heart rate monitor for forty-eight hours it turned out that my heart had only twenty ectopic beats in a total of 100,000 per day. Why was I worrying? Perhaps this was a sign of my self-induced status as one of the 'worried well'. Another entry in my health spreadsheet and back to normal life. Of course, normal life was by now unbelievably busy, as my angel investing career really took flight, while I continued to ski, hike and travel with Alison, with the boys and with friends.

Then I had a DVT scare, which was particularly frightening as this was what Christine had died from nine years earlier. A strange and quite intense pain in my knee led me to our local A&E a few hours after we landed in the UK on our return from Perth in Australia via Singapore – twenty hours in the air. Triage said a DVT, as did the blood test, so blood thinners were rapidly introduced. Then a registrar saw me and used an ultrasound to find that I had something called a Baker's cyst – a harmless fluid-filled growth behind the knee – which had probably burst. Phew...

Meanwhile, Alan moved out of home to be with friends close to his university in Cambridge. He said there were pros and cons of being a mature student at twenty-six: his classmates seemed very immature and he mixed little with most of them, but his dedication to coursework meant that he had time for a busy social life and still get a First on graduation.

Matt had a third operation on his ankle, which was more successful and hence allowed him to plan a working trip to Australia. However, he had to work through some very painful and difficult times in the continuing saga of his ankle first, one of which was that his two Swiss insurance companies, general health versus accident, both denied liability and he was stuck in the middle. One said his problem was due to a congenital defect, which to some extent it was, and the other said it was an accident, which it definitely was. In the end, one backed down and he got his pay-out.

I was proud of him, not just because he coped with the uncertainty and the pain, but for living in Geneva with friends and working in an office when he should have been in the mountains. Matt was due to fly out to Sydney to teach English as a Foreign Language, another skill he'd developed, later in 2014. He would go on to cycle from there to Melbourne (a wild 1,000km road trip) and then move to Byron Bay to work and live with his girlfriend in a campervan.

Shortly before he left, the three of us, Alan, Matt and I, spent Christmas at our new house in the French Alps, before we were joined by Alison and her family. The purchase of this house came about as a result of a trip I'd made with my parents more than ten years earlier. I'd gone with them to a town on the border of Spain and Portugal on the Bay of Cadiz to look for a property we could jointly purchase, to use as a holiday home. My parents would have spent more time there than us, but they couldn't afford to buy a four-bedroom house on their own, so the plan was to join forces. We had a lovely time together – it had been many years since I had spent time with them without kids in tow. However, our tastes differed. I wanted to buy a house in the town, with restaurants and shops within walking distance, whereas they wanted a new house on a housing estate with onsite parking. We looked at several houses through an estate agent, but we could not agree on a specific house. They then decided to move to the area for a couple of months in the winter and rent a house so they had the warmer weather without a commitment. In the end, my mother's deteriorating health meant the plan to co-own a property abroad never happened.

However, this had triggered a desire in me to buy a holiday home. Alison and I discussed this and decided on France and in particular, the Pyrenees. After some research, we found a townhouse in Prades, which is a town about 50km from

Perpignan airport and the Mediterranean coast, and less than 25km from two small ski resorts. It had a nice garden and was five minutes from the railway station.

In France one commits to buy (exchange contracts) many months before completing the purchase. So we'd exchanged, but not completed or taken possession, when Alan and I went to hike in Andorra. This was only 125km from the house in Prades and we therefore decided to visit the sellers, in the house, on the way, to learn about all the quirks and faults.

Our trip to Andorra was delayed by a funeral, as a few days before we flew, a close friend called Nat Billington died. Nat had taught me more about angel investing than any other person. He was fifteen years younger than me, but we had both studied Computer Science at Cambridge. He had then taken a year out while he and a friend, Lorenzo, built a startup, a digital marketing agency, which they sold. He then built another business in medical education which he also sold and he became an angel investor at about the same time as I did, concentrating in his case on carbon reduction technologies – 'cleantech' was the abbreviation in those days.

Nat and I had visited Alex and Toby, the founders of Vantage Power, together a few years earlier. Initially we were rather cynical, but after investment, we both joined the board. In 2015, we were having a pizza in my old home town of Stamford after looking at a potential investment in small wind turbines, when he said he had a pain in his back that was worrying him. This turned out to be lymph system cancer and he died twenty months later, leaving behind a wife and two teenage boys. I saw him as often as I could, including three weeks before he died.

At his funeral, Lorenzo gave a eulogy containing these words:

"When he received his first diagnosis of lymphoma, he tackled it with the same rigour and focus and calm optimism he had demonstrated in the rest of his life. I have not met anyone who knew him when he was ill who wasn't struck by how upbeat he was; how expert he became in his disease and its treatment; and how he remained thoroughly interested in how everyone else was doing, continuing to be a networker, a mentor and a loving husband and father throughout."

There is no doubt that spending time with Nat in those last months had a significant impact on me and my attitude, later on, to my own disease, in terms of acceptance of the situation and its inevitability, using a research-based approach to dealing with it, and living life to the full.

Once back from Andorra, I decided to take up a new sport. After forty-five years of playing squash, for many of which I had been overweight, my medial meniscus was torn. A couple of friends had introduced me to real tennis ('real' as in 'royal'), so I decided to take lessons. Real tennis evolved from an earlier ball game played around the 12th century in France, where the ball was hit with a bare hand and later a glove. By the 16th century the glove had become a racket. Real tennis later evolved into lawn tennis. It is almost always played indoors, with a net, but the court has pitched roofs, windows and doors (covered with netting so the ball doesn't injure spectators). There are fewer than fifty courts in the whole world.

After graduating, Alan joined a large consumer market research company in west London, living with a friend, but this didn't really suit him, as the friend worked long hours, and Alan didn't have many other friends in London. More importantly, he met and fell in love with a woman in Cambridge called Tasha and he was therefore commuting up and down at weekends. Tasha was Head of Department at a private school in Cambridge, that taught on Saturday mornings, which was inconvenient for a new relationship.

I had a couple of hiking adventures, climbing to the top of Mount Canigou (2,800m/9,000 feet) behind our house in Prades with friends for my 61st birthday, and walking the Coast to Coast long-distance footpath. This takes around a fortnight, is around 190 miles/300km and crosses the English Lake District, Pennines and Moors. There were four of us: Maggi, a close friend from Stamford and two friends of hers from Virginia: Ronnie, who had been recently diagnosed with cancer, and her husband, who drove rather than walked and was the most Republican of any American I have ever met, and ever hope to meet.

In 2016, Alison and I visited Laos and Vietnam, around the time of our anniversary of being together. On the actual day, on a rocking hammock in Hoi An, we decided to get married. We had been together for fifteen years and lived together for eleven of those. As it turned out, that marriage lasted for only two years, which is a source of much discussion both in my head and amongst family and friends.

As we were discussing it, we asked ourselves why should we get married, when we had been living together for so long? Was it necessary? Would it change our relationship? One aspect of the decision was that we had a complex and intertwined financial relationship, so there were significant tax advantages to being married if one of us died. The possibility of one of us dying seemed closer at that point than at other times in our life together, since Alison had had two different health issues and I was both overweight and incredibly busy, although I only felt stressed when late for a meeting or catching a train or plane.

In any case, it was an excuse for a party. We decided that it would just be family, and on an island. This island had to be within the UK so that Alison's mother Jean could join us. Alison's brother had been in a wheelchair for many years with multiple sclerosis, so found it very difficult to travel.

So, an island in the UK, not too far from London where Jean lived. There were about eight choices with the potential for a wedding, but there were only eight of us: Alison (whose mum couldn't come in the end), me, my two children, her three children and her eldest son's wife, whereas most venues had a minimum charge for thirty or even fifty guests.

In the end, we decided on a Victorian fort in the Solent that had been built to defend the UK from the French and had been converted to a hotel. But not everyone was comfortable in the small boat needed to get there, nor the alternative, a helicopter. Maybe even more importantly, the celebrant had to travel from the Isle of Wight. What would happen if it was too rough to get there? So for one of the few times in my life, we took out optional insurance, which was not needed as the seas were calm.

The whole family spent some time at Goodwood beforehand and competing in escape room sessions. All of the family had roles in the wedding ceremony and straight afterwards we got changed and played Laser Quest in the dimly lit deck of the fort where the cannonballs used to be stored. Being round, mirrors were strategically placed so that one could fire a laser via a mirror at an opponent who was hidden from view – my best wedding thus far!

* * * * *

Alan and Tasha decided to buy a house in a town just north of Cambridge called Waterbeach, and Alison and I had decided to give all our five children enough money to enable them to put a deposit on a house or further their education. We were the baby boomer generation and made money on housing, plus both of us were earning well.

Despite his ankylosing spondylitis, Alan joined two friends to cycle from Land's End to John O'Groats in eight days. LeJoG, as it's affectionately known, is a 1,200 mile/1,900km cycle ride from the very south of England to the northernmost point of mainland Scotland. I was very proud of Alan, especially with his degenerative condition. It was an incredible achievement for all three of them.

He moved back to Cambridge and moved in with us, together with Tasha, whilst their new house was being built. This was easier for Alan to do but more difficult for Tasha, who hadn't lived with an older generation for many years. They both coped very well. Alan started doing a master's degree in Agricultural Economics at SOAS with a dream of working overseas, perhaps in Uganda again.

In the meantime, I was still working hard as an angel investor (although it never felt like work) and plenty of interesting travel with Alison, including Myanmar, Prague, Sri Lanka, Guatemala and Costa Rica, as well as time at the house in Prades.

However, my father had retired from being a dentist on his 60th birthday, and my 65th birthday was now just a couple of years away, so I started to think about what retirement would mean for me. I had really enjoyed almost all of my life and had had a portfolio career for nearly twenty-five years, so adjusting to that seemed much easier to me than retirement from a single role/career that my father and many of my contemporaries had.

We had helped all three of Alison's children and Alan buy houses, but Matt decided to further his education. He wanted to undertake a five-month sailing training course in South Africa. This he did, attaining his Yachtmaster Ocean certificate, although he had to endure some challenges such as a storm almost pushing them onto rocks and the keel of the training yacht becoming loose shortly before attempting a crossing of the Atlantic. The crossing was delayed for several weeks as the course provider got hold of another yacht. Losing a keel at sea is very commonly a fatal accident.

Alan and Tasha had moved into their new house and Alison's children had also flown the nest. This meant that we were now officially empty-nesters and the house seemed too large. We intended to move from our village just outside Cambridge to Cambridge itself. We couldn't agree on where, so thought we'd sell the house and rent for a while whilst we worked it out. With two busy lives, it was a slow process, with the aim of putting the house on the market early the next year. It was not just recycling and gifting some of the clutter, but painting and mending the house so it was fit to sell.

I also decided to change cars once more. Porsche had contacted me offering to buy my Cayman at quite a lot more than what I thought it was worth, so I looked at hatchbacks with around the same power and swapped the Porsche for an Audi RS3. This is a small family hatchback with a very powerful engine, what the British call a Q-car and the Americans call a sleeper. This was much more practical, and although it looked fairly innocuous, a technical compromise on the sports exhaust meant it was very noisy when one started the car – annoyingly loud when leaving home early in the morning. And that car was astonishingly fast, but only in a straight line. Unlike Porsches, the RS3 is not keen on going around corners at speed.

As the idea of retiring in some way was maturing in my mind, I made the decision to run the last of six biennial dinners at my college for undergraduates and graduates who had studied Computer Science or were working in IT. We always had a guest speaker, and I decided to be the last one before handing over the baton. There were quite a number of people with dietary restrictions and I made life quite difficult for the catering staff by moving guests around between courses (a sort of musical chairs) so that every one of the approximately fifty people sat close to everyone else at some point. This year I labelled each seat with a number in Arabic and asked guests to move seven places clockwise. Chaos ensued, but it meant many new connections were made.

From the outside, our life was proceeding perfectly well. As a family, we had not had a major traumatic event for some years. Alison and I both enjoyed our work, we had fabulous foreign travel together and there were no worries about the children. But in reality, we were drifting apart. We were not arguing, but spending very little time together in the house unless we had friends round for dinner or to play bridge. We shared a love of holidays, except skiing and mountain hiking, which I did with friends.

I spent many hours agonising about what to do. Alison was comfortable and appeared accepting of our lives and lifestyle. She enjoyed her work as a senior accountant, her bridge (although we rarely played together as a partnership, because of my work commitments), her badminton and our large group of shared friends. But I wanted more. A new challenge? The intense love of a new relationship? It didn't help matters that I had become close, too close, to a colleague called Belinda.

I spent a long time working out whether, if I was to leave Alison, I didn't mind being single. I could certainly cope with life as I had occasionally been single after separating from Christine. And I decided with the help of a therapist that I could cope and that my life would be more what I wanted.

Whether this is right or wrong, I decided not to ask Alison whether she would attend marriage counselling with me. I made a unilateral decision that we should go our separate ways.

Chapter 15
A New Chapter

After the breakup, in January 2019, Alison stayed in the house in Harston. We arranged to split everything fifty-fifty, including future investment outcomes. Our finances were closely entangled so the process of setting this all up was lengthy and complicated. I moved out to a rented flat near Cambridge station, which I soon came to adore. It was on two upper floors of a converted heritage-listed Victorian flour mill, with a living space, one bedroom and a large office and two balconies, one of which overlooked the busy Cambridge railway station. From locking the apartment door to boarding a train took little more than five minutes and I could cycle into the centre of town in the same time. My two main rail destinations, London and Stansted Airport, were both forty-five minutes by train. I had planned to move on one particular Sunday, and my friend Brian came to help, but it was not easy, as the lift was broken that day and we had to carry everything up about ten flights of stairs. That was exhausting and we soon gave up and reconvened the following weekend, hiring the van again, when the lift was operational.

After completing his Yachtmaster course in 2019 Matt came back to Europe to work in Geneva and look for a sailing job in Mallorca. Later that year, he took a cruise to Brazil with 250 entrepreneurs and 'digital nomads'. But towards the end of the year, I had a difficult telephone conversation with him. He was struggling with me and our relationship. He told me that he felt I showed no interest in him and didn't listen to him. I was surprised, concerned and shocked. My idea of what our relationship was like was so different from his. After the phone call I had little communication from him for many months.

By this time, Belinda and I had become a couple and began to build a life together, and although she lived in Bury St Edmunds, about an hour away, she worked in Cambridge for the Cambridge University Judge Business School, where she ran their social venture programme as both an entrepreneur and an academic. She has three children and they stayed with their dad for about half the time, which meant Belinda would stay over in Cambridge during the week and I spent many weekends in Bury St Edmunds. Her children were about fifteen years younger than mine, but I enjoyed getting to know and spending time with all of them.

Although Belinda and I shared similar family values, and were both passionate about entrepreneurship, we had some pretty major differences. Since coming out of childhood, my politics had gradually moved left of centre after long discussions with my aunt in Australia and with my close friend David, the son of a Durham miner. I generally voted for personalities rather than parties in local elections, and in national elections swung between Liberal Democrat and Labour, voting for Tony Blair but not Jeremy Corbyn, who was too far left for me. Belinda also passionately supported transgender and non-binary people, whom I learnt about and accepted. You could say that I became 'woke'.

Belinda was a Corbyn supporter, thought that neo-liberalism was damaging the world, and was pretty anti-capitalism, so to some extent, I represented the 'enemy' – an older, white, privileged, wealthy male. Our discussions were quite robust!

With encouragement and support from Belinda, I started changing my life – I worked considerably less (my number of sent emails that year went down by 35%), took up running and significantly reduced my calorie intake, which led to me losing 21kg that year alone (about 18% of my body weight).

The weight loss was somewhat helped by ten days in southern Germany at a therapeutic fasting clinic, consuming 250 calories a day, whilst using up about 5,000 calories exercising. The clinic organises two-hour walks every morning and many events and activities throughout the day, such as yoga. I also ran 5km every other day. A single cashew nut broke the week-long ketosis and I had permanently lost 5kg.

As for the running, I was sixty-four years old when I took it up, and, as so often when people first start, hated it with a vengeance for about a month before it clicked and I gradually increased my monthly total from 50km to over 100km. I discovered Parkrun (all over the world 350,000 people walk and run 5km on a Saturday morning at free events, supported by sponsor organisations and facilitated by volunteers) and entered the Cambridge Half Marathon, which was only seven months after I started running. Why had I not discovered running earlier in my life?

Alan and Tasha had got engaged on a Pyrenean ski slope, planning to get married in mid-2020. But Alan was struggling with the way that I had left Alison. He felt we should have gone through a process of trying to repair the marriage rather than me just abandoning it. And because we needed to spend several hours a week together on The Invested Investor, Tasha suggested joint counselling. Alan had had a small number of sessions after his mother died and I had had at least one hundred sessions over the previous two decades and was very positive about the benefits.

We found an excellent therapist in Cambridge, who found the blockage between us within three or four ninety-minute sessions. When Alison and I split up, Alan blamed me for doing it in an upsetting and clumsy way, which after counselling, he then accepted was down to my human fallibility. The therapist asked me a question in such a way that I said something which I should have worked out for myself, but hadn't. She said: "Peter, are you sure you were thinking clearly when you decided to separate from Alison?" I said: "No, I'm sure I was so emotionally upset by it that I wasn't." She didn't exactly put the words into my mouth, but my reply demonstrated to Alan that I was more prone to making mistakes than he'd imagined. After the counselling sessions our relationship became much better. Alan continued alone with this therapist for a while working through his mother's and brother's deaths and his childhood.

I continued to travel extensively, including to Canada in late spring of 2019. There we visited a friend of Belinda's who lived on Manitoulin Island, which is the largest island on a freshwater lake in the world. Later, we went to New England for the fall, plus I made work trips to Qatar (in 53°C heat) and Tunis (where Belinda and I learnt a huge amount about the Maghreb) and I spoke in many countries around Europe.

August 2019 saw the tenth anniversary of Ian's death, so Belinda and I spent a few days in and around Glastonbury, where he last lived, and, with a group of his friends, spread more ashes from the Tor. There were only a dozen of us, and the conversation was intense, hearing again how much Ian had positively affected their lives.

In the autumn I spent five days hiking between Pyrenean huts with university friends, Chris and Geoff.

Belinda and I planned to travel the world in 2020 on a 'gap year', which was also intended to act as a transition to a slower life for me. The gap year would be 'slow travel', visiting a few places for an extended time and not worrying if one missed the bus and had to remain somewhere interesting or beautiful for another week. But of course, when 2020 came round, so did the coronavirus pandemic.

Not long before the first Covid lockdown I ran my first half marathon, the Cambridge Half. I had been doing longer and longer runs, up to around 18km (a half marathon is 21km) but struggled with boredom after about 15km, despite listening to podcasts and audiobooks. Luckily, organised events allow bone conduction earphones (so one can still hear course marshals and the surroundings) and I had been introduced to them by a local entrepreneur, who had invented a system to help children with glue ear.

This was the 9th of March and there was some pressure to cancel it, and who knows whether it would have been classed as a 'superspreader' event, but I really enjoyed it. I decided early not to resort to walking, although my running pace slackened. The Cambridge course is mainly pretty and interesting, going through some Cambridge colleges, except it has a long haul along a road out to the M11 motorway junction and back.

My time was two hours and ten minutes, where I had expected around two and half hours. Was I now a real runner, despite my age?

Two weeks later, Belinda and I decided to celebrate twenty years since I had last drunk alcohol and go away for the weekend to the Cotswolds. Looking back on it, it was not the best idea to go ahead with that, as in-person events were being cancelled and almost all meetings replaced with Zoom. We went anyway, but at breakfast on the Saturday, the hotel said all residents had to leave that morning as the government shut all hospitality venues. We found a local Airbnb at short notice and then stayed a further night near London.

The roads were quiet as we drove back to Cambridge on the 23rd of March and that evening, the Cambridge Angels had a pitch for a novel form of ventilator, which I believe didn't get to market. At 8pm, I was on an emergency board call for one of my investments – the Dogtooth strawberry-picking robot – and watching the Prime Minister, Boris Johnson, on one of my other screens, giving a speech with a sombre face. That was on mute, so I was also watching the BBC News timeline text. When lockdown was announced, I excused myself from the board meeting and rang Belinda as we had to make a rapid decision.

We were told no unnecessary travel from midnight that day, and we had to decide whether I was going to live for perhaps months alone in my flat or live with her and her family in Bury St Edmunds. We chose the latter.

I rapidly filled the car with what I needed and drove the twenty-five miles to her home, and in the middle of the night I woke and realised I had forgotten my laptop charger, so dashed back for that and a few more bits. In fact, the rules were not legally introduced for a few more days and so I returned for my bicycle later in the week.

I was lucky. I am not good at being by myself, and no one knew for how long the lockdown would be. It turned out to be a long three months, and Belinda and her family were very homely and supportive.

I got to know and love Bury St Edmunds well, cycling and running every day. The weather was unusually good that spring in the UK. My days were full of video calls, and my evenings social calls and TV. I had planned and booked trips to Japan, the English Lakes, Ireland, the USA, France and Spain, which all evaporated. I learnt how to play bridge online with a group of friends but struggled with working out whether an entrepreneurial team was investable on Zoom. I found team dynamics particularly difficult to observe and analyse.

My appearances on *The Naked Scientists* programme continued in the BBC studio and this meant that as a 'journalist' I was allowed to travel to work along a very empty dual carriageway.

Matt was in Manaus, deep in the Amazonian jungle, in mid-March and caught one of the last flights out to lock down with a friend in Sussex.

Hotels reopened on the 4th of July 2020, so Belinda and I went to a hotel in Norfolk, where the staff and guests were trying to work out how to interpret the government's confusing rules using plastic screens, wooden cutlery and plates.

We also went to the fasting clinic again, jumping through the various Covid testing and isolation hoops needed to enter Germany and then return to the UK. Whilst we were there, Alan and Tasha got legally married in London, with both families attending by Zoom. We were asked to keep quiet about that, as the celebration with family and friends was to be postponed for a year.

Matt lived and worked in Europe during the summer and then worked on farms in Portugal to get residency and hence free movement within the EU, as the UK finally Brexited at the end of 2020. We started to rebuild our relationship, as he felt that I was changing for the better. I was working less hard, had more time for relationships, was less stressed. He approved of the fact that, under the influence of Belinda, I had learned to cook, had taken up exercise and lost weight. Nonetheless, I saw him only once in 2020, just for a few hours.

I also went out to the house in France to check it was okay and do some hiking in the Pyrenees. Returning meant an enforced quarantine period at my flat, alone for a few days. Then followed a period of relative normality with some in-person meetings and some remaining via video calls. I hiked in Derbyshire and Snowdonia (Eryri) with friends, and although Covid was still a huge issue around the world and we were all fearing the disease once we moved back to an indoor life in winter, I was lucky enough to have had a good summer.

Meanwhile, Alison and I had put our joint home on the market and sold it for a price, which, allowing for inflation, was similar to what we had paid for it sixteen years earlier. I was already renting at this point, and I had not decided whether to ever buy a house again. But I did investigate that option, only to find that I would not be able to get an interest-only mortgage after the age of sixty-five, which was in a few weeks' time. If I was going to take on a mortgage again, I would have to do it at double speed.

You may ask why take out a mortgage at all, at sixty-five? I wanted to keep plenty of cash available and was pretty certain I could pay off the mortgage with exits. I started looking at houses and found a place I liked, just within the few weeks I had left before my birthday, and decided on a five-year fixed rate. Once interest rates started going up, I would be making money by earning more from the cash than I was paying on the mortgage. Although my father never had to learn much about personal finances, I was pleased to find that he still had a mortgage when he died at eighty-six. It meant that he could continue to live somewhat beyond what his pension would allow, by releasing equity.

I settled on a ten-year-old three-storey house in a mostly Victorian area of Cambridge, close to Fitzwilliam College where I had studied. Unusually, this residential house was owned by one of the Cambridge colleges, which had used it for postgraduate student accommodation. I'd completed over twenty house sales and purchases over the years and this was the most unusual. As far as they were concerned it was not a house but an asset that needed selling. This meant no emotional connection and a very easy ride for me. All the minor faults in the house were fixed by them, and they didn't provide the 'fixtures and fittings' form, as they said I would simply get the key and I would then own whatever was in the now empty house.

It has all the advantages of being in a Victorian part of the city, yet is only a few years old, with a very practical design, lots of light and energy efficiency and five minutes' cycle from the city centre.

As described earlier, Belinda and I had our differences and there had to be give and take, as in any relationship. But in late October, just before I was about to move, Belinda video-called me and said that some of our values were too different for her and that we could not continue in a relationship. We met a few days later to talk it through and it was clear that her decision was final. Although I knew we had our differences, this came as a complete shock to me.

The removal company was booked for me to move into my new house on the 5th of November, one day before the UK government enforced a second lockdown. Luckily house moves were excluded from the restrictions, so my possessions from both the apartment and from the family home were moved into my new house that week and I was newly single. In the evening, I went out to a local discount supermarket, miserably buying a meal for one.

I had hoped to be walking with a group on Gran Canaria from Boxing Day, although that was cancelled four days beforehand as the world settled into a Covid-infused winter.

And what of my plans to travel around the world with Belinda? Clearly that would not now happen and thus I replanned the next few years of my life.

I watched far too much television and, although I played a lot of online bridge and did a lot of online cryptic crosswords, for the first time in my life I felt lonely. I had a dozen Zoom meetings per day, but the nights were dark and long and, except within my bubble (a UK government-defined artefact) I really missed human interaction, and of course physical contact and intimacy.

So I ventured back into online dating (no, not Tinder!) with an open mind, as twenty years before, I'd met Alison on a dating website. This led to meeting several women, one of whom has become a close non-romantic friend.

One woman strongly stood out – Liesbeth, and we started the courting process via outdoor walks and picnics, which Liesbeth called 'corona dates'. It was unusual as we couldn't go into each other's homes and had to stay two metres apart, but over a few weeks, we became close. Liesbeth was born in the Netherlands and had been in the UK for over thirty years. I learned that she had a PhD in medieval English and that she worked as a freelance translator, so there was no overlap in our backgrounds! But that didn't matter. We had similar values and a shared love of hiking, skiing, and travel, although I don't share her love of singing (nor the arts in general). And we are both very open, forthright and direct. We had so much to talk about every time we met.

Alan and Tasha and their two Labradors moved from a village just north of Cambridge to a few miles south, with a little help from the Bank of Dad. Their new home was on the edge of a village, with fields and hills for the dogs. Tasha was promoted to Deputy Head at her school in Cambridge and Alan to a more senior role at Martlet Capital. Alan and Tasha finally had a really wonderful wedding celebration at Holkham Hall on the Norfolk coast. Liesbeth and I got to drive the hired Morgan wedding car to the location, but of course Tasha's father was the one to drive his daughter to the wedding venue in this beautiful vehicle on the day. Although the Morgan motor company used to have a ten-year waiting list from order to delivery, I really don't know why; the steering is incredibly heavy and the soft top leaked when it rained. I think I have become too accustomed to modern cars. However, we did stir up some interest in the campsite where we stayed on one of the nights – in a downpour as it happens.

As Covid gradually transitioned to a less dangerous threat and most of the UK population had been vaccinated, I went on several hiking trips in the UK, the Alps and the Pyrenees. I significantly improved my running too, driven partly by weight loss, partly by being fitter and mostly as I love seeing the progress on my spreadsheet!

Now that I had reached sixty-five, as planned some years before, I gradually unwound more roles and still intended to travel for many months once Covid allowed. I 'Zoom lectured' in many more countries and cities, including North Macedonia, Alexandria, Armenia, Qatar and even Iran.

Matt came back to the UK for Alan and Tasha's wedding in the summer of 2021. On the way back from Portugal, Matt had a month in the Pyrenees, partly with me, but alone when he climbed 3,000m and walked 44km in a single day to the top of our local peak, Mount Canigou. Once back in the UK, he took a full-time role at Tasha's school with both classroom and extra-curricular duties such as teaching climbing, sailing and paddleboarding.

We'd mostly rebuilt our relationship, so we were both a bit worried when he moved in (at my suggestion) with me, but it didn't take long to enjoy living together. It was a real privilege to live with an independent adult child, in this era of boomerang kids.

The house in Prades had finally found a committed buyer after being on the market for two years. It had been a great place, but for obvious reasons had hardly been used in the previous couple of years.

Camdata remained a profitable but small business and, now that Alan worked for Martlet, even The Invested Investor company was profitable, since Alan was drawing a much smaller salary out of it. I had several more complete write-offs of my angel investments and, comfortingly, a few angel investment exits. The biggest of these was Arachnys, where I had backed the founder David Buxton since the first funding round about nine years earlier, being the investor director for most of that time. I had invested in five separate funding rounds and it was the biggest investment I ever made. It was on this board that I realised that I am of use during the startup phase of a company but not during the scale-up phase. The exit comprised a return on our cash investment and I exercised my share options and received a decent amount of money for all the time I had helped David build the company. I had the opportunity to sell all my shares for cash or roll some over as shares in the acquiring company, which I did, hoping they would be worth more as the combined companies grew over the following years.

As with the Vantage Power and James and James exits, where I had no further interaction with the company, I was sad not to spend time with David and Arachnys any longer. But this illustrates the life cycle of an angel-backed company. One is involved from near its birth to either its death (as a failure) or its rebirth as part of a bigger organisation, or on a stock market.

Juggling ever-changing Covid travel rules, Liesbeth and I visited her mother and brother in the Netherlands, but got refused boarding on the Eurostar on the way back, as the Dutch government test centre had not included the PCR test manufacturer's name on the test certificate (!), a rule that had been brought in the evening before our travel. This was not that much hassle for us as we could continuing staying with Liesbeth's family, but there were many very upset passengers on the platform with the same problem.

We celebrated my 66th birthday in Paris, with one day chosen by me (3-star Michelin restaurant and a film at an Art Deco cinema) and one by Liesbeth (Musée d'Orsay), where she very patiently tried to explain and educate me in the wonders of looking at and enjoying art, although unfortunately unsuccessfully.

All this time, I was still considering how to shape the next decade of my life, as I was nearing 'retirement', whatever that would mean for me. At one point I put a great deal of effort into applying for a year's course (The Distinguished Careers Institute) at Stanford University in California which two friends had recommended, but I was rejected. I then looked into doing a UK university Professional Doctorate and decided that analysing my career highlights using an academic lens was well outside my comfort zone, so backed out. Instead, I started two part-time second-year Open University degree courses, Human Biology and Astronomy.

In November of 2021, I managed to run my second half marathon of the year. I shaved 3% off my 'Personal Best', although that saving of four minutes in just over two hours was very tough! Alan accompanied me for some of the race and over the line, although he could have been half an hour in front of me if he wanted. It's one of my most special memories of my time with Alan.

In hindsight, it is quite astonishing to think I was running at all, considering what was going on in my body. By the 30th of December, I'd been given a diagnosis of Stage IV lung cancer.

Chapter 16
Facing the Diagnosis

At the consultation on the 30th of December 2021, described right at the start of this story, when I first found out that I had lung cancer, the respiratory consultant explained that a biopsy needed to be done to find out exactly which mutation I had. He expected to find a non-small cell lung cancer of a type that non-smokers often get. I've smoked probably about twenty-five cigarettes in my entire life, mostly when tipsy in my twenties. There is a large amount of stigma and an unfair blame culture attached to lung cancer – the idea that you have brought it upon yourself if you have been a smoker. It is completely unfair to treat lung cancer patients differently from anyone else with a disease. Who amongst us lives a life where they don't take any risks with their health at all, ever? Quite apart from this stigma, it is a fact that this disease can strike anyone, and up to 20% of lung cancer patients have never smoked.

After that first diagnosis, we were simply reeling from the shock of finding out how serious and how advanced the cancer was. Going home in a daze I had two things on my mind: I wanted to find out as much as I possibly could about my disease and treatment options. I live on data and a factual approach to life. I knew that for me the best way to come to terms with what was happening was to gather data, data, data, to keep as much control as I possibly could over my life, my body and what was going to happen to it, and in the short term to not let the cancer and its treatment take over my life any more than it needed to. The other thing on my mind was: face the reality. If I only had a short time to live, what did I want to do with that time?

My medical team set out to discover the genetic make-up of my cancer, which would determine what treatment was available. At the start of January, I returned to hospital for a biopsy to be taken of lymph node tissue. It was explained to me that histological and DNA analysis would be carried out that would take around two to three weeks to yield a result. This seemed a very long time, but then everything does at this stage in the diagnostic period. Nothing goes fast enough when you have been told you may have a life-threatening disease. You feel in limbo. In any case, it was a relief to me to know that my tissue was now at least 'in the system'.

We started another period of waiting. However, 'waiting' was not the focus of our days. I believe in using one's time proactively and constructively, even more so in this situation where all we could do, in terms of my health situation, was to keep taking the steroids to reduce the swelling around the larger tumour in my brain which was now 27mm across, and wait for test results. We had already decided to go on a trip around the UK to see a number of people who have been and still are important to me. For Liesbeth that was a super-charged introduction to the sixty-five years of my life before we knew each other. For me it was a wonderful way to connect once more, for perhaps the last time as I inevitably couldn't help thinking, with people from different parts of my life. We went to visit Chris, the first friend I met when I started university in 1974, with whom I'd run the travelling disco. We also made a pilgrimage to see the place on the Bristol Channel where Ian died, and we went to Oxford, to see friend and business life coach Katy and her family.

After these trips, just ten days after the shocking appointment with the respiratory consultant at the end of December, we were ushered into the consulting room of the oncologist who remains my main doctor until the present day. He works both in the NHS and privately and since I'm lucky enough to be able to use private treatment if necessary, on this occasion we saw him in his private consulting room in Cambridge.

We entered the consultant's room quite apprehensively, and both vaguely noted the presence of another person in the room, which Liesbeth immediately registered as a red flag – probably someone to offer support. David, the oncologist, was very calm and careful in his attitude and told us that the tissue taken from the lymph node was not useable. This did not sound good to us. However, he went on to say that a genetic analysis of the cancer DNA circulating in the blood showed that my cancer was, to give it its full title: T2N2M1C in the right upper lobe; adenocarcinoma; EGFR+ EXON 19 mutation. As had been expected, this is one of the types of lung cancer that non-smokers can get. Fortunately for me, this is a mutation that can be detected by a blood test – not all types can be diagnosed this way. He explained that a new drug had been approved for use in the UK relatively recently, and that he was going to recommend it for my treatment.

"It is a highly targeted therapy called osimertinib, and is taken as a tablet at home just once a day. It is what's called a tyrosine kinase inhibitor. It alters the cells to stop them reproducing, so the tumours can't expand, and gradually die off."

He went on to explain that it had been found to be highly effective for as long as the cancer didn't mutate. Liesbeth and I looked at each other. What exactly did he mean? Were we looking at more than a few months of life expectancy?

He went on: "To be exact, 20% of patients don't respond to it at all. Sometimes patients have side-effects that can be severe enough that we have to pause or stop treatment. But many patients benefit for many months, sometimes years. The positive effects should start within six to twelve weeks."

We could barely believe what he was saying. It was a no-brainer. Of course I was going to try anything that would give me more time.

"In most cases, the cancer will mutate at some point, after perhaps ten to twenty-four months, and escape from the drug. But then other therapies are available."

"Do you have health insurance? Do you want to pay for it yourself?" he asked.

"Well," I said, "how much is it?"

"Five thousand pounds a month."

"I don't have health insurance and I've paid tax all my life. Can I have it on the NHS?"

"Of course," came the answer.

We came out of the building stunned, but this time we were stunned for different reasons. Liesbeth was completely elated, laughing and crying and full of hope and joy. But as we were driving away, I said to her: "But I don't believe it. I don't trust it. I have seen many mistaken diagnoses and things gone wrong in healthcare, I just don't believe it." And that is how I felt. I could not allow myself to get carried away and to believe what he said was really true. They'd probably find there'd been a mistake or something and we'd be back to square one.

But as the days went on, the incredible news began to sink in. What I wanted now was to get on with the treatment, and hope that it was going to work for me. I knew that only after the first few months and then only after scan evidence of the drug working would I be able to really start to accept that I might have a lot longer left to live than I had first thought.

After some more blood tests and an ECG, I started taking osimertinib, nicknamed 'osi' by EGFR+ patients, on the 19th of January 2022. I was put on a schedule of monthly checkups with the oncologist, where we would discuss any side-effects or other issues and he would prescribe the next month's supply of the drug. I'd have MRI and CT scans every three months, to see whether and how the drug was working, by measuring the size of the various tumours.

Meanwhile, I started to act on the assumption that I would not have to 'hand over my life' to the NHS in the short term, and that I could work on a two-year, rather than a three-month, life plan. I decided to continue seeing people that were important to me, and also to spend quality one-to-one time with Matt and Alan. With Matt, I went on a fantastic hiking weekend in the Peak District, where I made slow but happy progress up Kinder Scout and Alan and I spent a great weekend in London, going for dinner at Gordon Ramsay's restaurant, go-karting, seeing Monster Trucks at the O2 and visiting a comedy club. Liesbeth and I went off to Hull, in the second week of January 2022, for me to reminisce and see cousins and friends from that part of the country, generating lots of wonderful new memories.

I carried on reading about and researching my cancer, and found support groups in the UK and the USA who ran Facebook pages and newsletters. Liesbeth also found an organisation carrying out research and complementary treatments in London, the Care Oncology Clinic. I had a call with one of their doctors to talk through their treatment approach and did some of my own research on the organisation and what they were offering. As a result, I made a note to discuss with my oncologist whether it would be useful, or at least non-harmful, to add a drug called metformin to my treatment. This is a drug approved for diabetes, but there is some evidence that it can help slow down the rate at which the cancer mutates to the point where osimertinib is no longer effective.

I continued to be determined to not let the cancer or the treatment take over my life any more than absolutely necessary as we slowly started to get used to living with the diagnosis and finding our way of coping.

I also started to attend some sessions of the Alpha Course, which I had heard about through a friend and colleague, and which introduces the basics of the Christian faith through talks and discussions. I talked to three scientifically-minded friends who I respected and who had become Christian in their twenties – now that my life was likely to be foreshortened, I wondered if I could take solace in a belief in God. The three friends had all read C. S. Lewis and decided that if Jesus Christ was not bad nor mad, then the Bible was to be believed. I do believe in a higher power, but even after the course, on which I met many interesting people, I could not accept the resurrection of Christ.

On the physical side, I still had some of the balance issues caused by the tumour in my brain, and it was predicted that this problem would continue for a while until the drug started to work and that tumour would shrink (along with the others). I continued to play golf, spectacularly badly due to my unsteadiness, but with great gusto and enjoyment. I was gifted a trip in a Spitfire aeroplane by two friends, and so I secretly increased my steroid dose for a few days in order to be able to walk to the plane in a straight line and not be turned away by the pilot as unfit. An old university friend, who was on his own cancer journey, introduced me to the wonderful concept of the 'fuck-it list', for all the things you don't actually need to or want to do – the inverse of the bucket list. You might have guessed by now that I am a spreadsheet junkie and immediately started to keep both lists. I actually enjoy most of what I do, so I don't have any major items on this list, but it is still a useful concept for setting priorities, and seeing which activities I can scrap more easily than others.

After about a month, in mid-February, we made our first regular visit to the oncologist. We mostly discussed the side effects I was starting to experience, which were mainly skin-related and not too serious: dry skin, mouth ulcers, brittle nails. I had not yet managed to reduce the steroids down to zero, so there were still sleep problems and I was also quite short of breath. I felt my general health was deteriorating rather than improving. The oncologist told me to be patient, but he did order a chest X-ray to investigate the shortness of breath. Being patient is definitely not one of my core strengths and I class myself as an 'impatient patient'. I came to the consultation knowing that I had an invitation to speak on a panel in Paris for the European Research Council three weeks later. I was keen to go, and to let them know as soon as possible that I was coming. These are things I really enjoy doing, so I asked the oncologist if it was okay to travel.

"Well, it is probably a good idea to stay fairly close to home for the time being, to see how the treatment beds in."

"Mmm. I've heard what you've said, and I am going to Paris."

As we walked out of the hospital, Liesbeth was giggling next to me.

"Honestly, if you're going to ignore his advice, do you need to tell him to his face?"

As we talked it over, we decided that it was just a train ride, no further than somewhere in the UK, really, and we were going to manage. We planned to make a bit of a holiday out of it, with a trip to Reims as well as Paris.

Luckily, that same evening, I had a phone call from the hospital to say first of all that the shortness of breath was probably just due to weight gain caused by the steroids and secondly, that it looked as if the primary lung tumour was shrinking. Spectacular news.

The next couple of months saw a gradual improvement in my fitness and general physical condition. I could cycle again without danger of falling over, and I started to run again. The latter was really important, as I felt good fitness would make me better able to withstand aggressive treatment. I had booked a place to run the Cambridge Half Marathon again in March, but there was obviously no way I was going to be able to take part in that, so I transferred my place to Matt, who used it to run a very impressive one hour thirty-four minutes. I also worked on my weight. I had spent the previous three years losing 30kg, but the steroid treatment around the start of the year had caused significant weight gain. I wanted to get it all off again. I also continued to do the things I love: going to a Global Entrepreneurship Conference in Riyadh, having a weekend away with Alan and Matt on a narrowboat in Staffordshire, and taking a trip to La Gomera, one of the Canary Islands, with Liesbeth. We didn't quite think that one through, since it is a volcanic island and all the walks are steeply up and down. However, it gave us a lovely week away with warmth and sunshine.

Meanwhile, I had decided that my OU Astronomy course was interesting but the coursework was too theoretical, so I read the accompanying literature but didn't take the exam. However, the Human Biology course was both fascinating and appropriately timed – I had been learning about the brain when my brain tumour was discovered and soon moved onto the cancer module. I completed most of the coursework and studied hard for the exam. This was the last of the Covid online ones, which was by far the most relaxed I had ever taken. My desktop has three large monitors, so I could display the full coursework and Google whilst I wrote my answers in Word. We had been warned that our submission would be checked for plagiarism, so cutting and pasting was a complete no-no, and we had four hours to complete the exam: three hours for answering and one hour to upload (in case of connectivity issues). I loved answering the essay at the end. We were given the question 'Is stress essential for survival?' and my conclusion was that 'acute stress is essential for survival but chronic stress is detrimental'. I achieved the equivalent of a 2.2, which is what I deserved.

In April came the first quarterly check-up with scan results, and our first brush with 'scanxiety' (scan-related anxiety), something that many fellow cancer-sufferers are sadly familiar with. To our massive relief and delight, the scans showed that the tumours were indeed shrinking. The tumour in my brain had halved in each dimension, which means the volume had reduced by a factor of about eight, an incredible result.

This gave us the green light for a visit to New York where one of Liesbeth's closest friends lived, and I also had a second visit to Riyadh in Saudi Arabia to educate angel investors. I had a lot of time to talk to the citizens about their lives and I came back with a less black and white view about the role of women in Saudi Arabia than I had held previously – the ones I spoke to valued the separation of sexes in gyms and swimming pools and didn't feel oppressed. But perhaps this was due to conditioning, or to the privileged position in society that these women had. The fundamental issue remains that none of these rules or arrangements were made by women for themselves.

In May, Liesbeth and I spent a week in south-west Ireland touring the coast, hiking and boating before we reached Cork, where the annual conference of EBAN was being held – the first one in three years that was to take place in person. I was so pleased to meet many close colleagues and friends and gave a keynote speech on my angel investment exits. Completely out of the blue I won the award for the 'Best exit of a business funded by early-stage investors', for my investment and chairing the board of James and James (my 107 times angel return, you may remember).

I felt in the eye of the storm. Thanks to the drug, I was leading an almost normal life, with (fun) work, travel, exercise, normal sleeping and only minor side-effects, but always in the knowledge that the cancer would mutate 'away' from the drug in the next months or years and the storm would resume, perhaps with less gentle treatment.

I had been building up my activities with the various lung-cancer charities, and in July attended the British Thoracic Oncology Group conference in London with the EGFR+ patient charity chair and her husband. We were representing patient interests, together with about a dozen others. The conference was encouraging due to the huge amount of research, progress and strong collaboration taking place at all levels in the NHS, yet also brought home once again the seriousness of my condition – many graphs showed mortality rates using various treatment options. At times it was easy to understand and at times it was, unsurprisingly, very technical. I had a long talk with my own oncologist, David, who is on the steering committee of this Group. After dinner, an 80s tribute pop band came on and everyone took to the dance floor, so Liesbeth and I had the surreal and thoroughly amusing experience of dancing with my oncologist.

Also in that summer, I received another award from the UKBAA. My Angel of the Year award had been eight years before and in July 2022, fellow Cambridge Angel and close friend Robert and I were awarded 'Exit of the Year' for backing David Buxton in Arachnys. Robert was a co-founder of the Cambridge Angels and had been instrumental in me becoming a member.

Liesbeth and I began to meet more and more of each other's friends and enjoy events together, like the Henley rowing regatta. I lectured in Lisbon, again on angel investment exits. I was starting to know a lot about these by now: because I have invested in so many companies (seventy-six) I was beginning to have more exits and failures than most angels have investments.

By this time, we were planning our life in three-monthly intervals bounded by the scan dates. After another set of positive results in June, we went on a road trip to Vienna via friends and family in the Netherlands and then hiked in the Hintertux, before visiting friends in Munich. August saw us at the Edinburgh Fringe and a few days on Orkney, a beautifully remote part of the UK.

Liesbeth went hiking in September with a friend and I helped one of my friends move his yacht from Norway to the Netherlands. Apart from a clumsy jump (all my own fault) in Bergen, which led to a year-long problem with plantar fasciitis (an injury to the base of the foot), I really enjoyed the daytime part of the trip. For instance, if I was not at the helm I was the only one of the four of us who could read a book on the choppy seas and my record of consuming books is very poor as I don't seem to prioritise reading. However, the overnight watches of four hours on, then four hours off duty made me realise that I am a day sailor rather than a long-distance sailor.

The crew were excellent company and the trip had an unexpected but wonderful side-effect. I had been seeing a neuro-oncology physiotherapist at my local hospital as my balance was still poor. She said this was due to my brain being permanently damaged as the big (27mm diameter) secondary tumour grew, and that my brain needed to rebuild electrical pathways. I was given exercises such as standing on one leg and walking with my eyes shut, but I always found these sort of exercises tedious, however sensible they were.

On the rolling decks of a yacht on the North Sea in a 22-knot strong breeze for two or three days, my brain was building new pathways like there was no tomorrow. After the trip, my balance was almost back to normal and I finished the programme with her.

I had also been hoping to visit Japan, with a close friend from university, Michael, but Japan was still not open to tourists, so we spent a week touring restaurants in Alsace. This helped with deciding how I want to spend time with very close friends and loved ones before I die.

The targeted therapy, osimertinib, was working incredibly well. All my tumours had shrunk so that most of them were invisible to the MRI and CT scanners, which is called 'No Evidence of Disease'. The ones that could be seen, mainly in the lung and bone, were almost certainly only visible because of dead cancer cells.

For my 67th birthday, we went out to dinner with Matt, his girlfriend, Alan and Tasha, which was a lovely evening and just a few days before Liesbeth and I set off on the first of several major holidays. I felt I was getting to grips with life after the diagnosis.

As things settled down, I started to wonder whether I could somehow share my experience of cancer for the benefit of others, as I had done with angel investing in the form of *The Invested Investor* book and podcasts.

Chapter 17

Project Cancer

I have always been and remain a very optimistic person. I believe in a positive outlook, in doing at least as much research as my medical team, in approaching my disease as dispassionately as possible, to rely on facts and data, to make the most of life while I can. Unlike my alcoholism and the deaths of loved ones I feel this is something I have a level of control over and I want to put that to good use. This is why, as I started to reach a plateau of general wellbeing as a result of the drug, I decided I wanted to share my experience far more widely. It could help someone else get diagnosed sooner. It could offer support and encouragement to someone newly diagnosed, and improve understanding and challenge misconceptions about lung cancer. I reckoned that if I could be open about my disease and treatment, it might help to reduce stigma and taboo, which would help everyone.

I had already been keeping a blog for all my existing friends and acquaintances, accessible with a password. In addition, I now decided to go completely public, and set up a YouTube channel called Project Cancer, a name I chose because I regard my cancer as a joint venture project with the NHS to keep me healthy and alive for as long as possible and because compared with Ian's death, cancer was of relatively less consequence. In this channel, I could post podcasts about my progress and about topics surrounding cancer, including interviews with fellow-patients, carers and professionals.

I had time to reflect on my own journey so far, and to talk to and learn from many others while interviewing them for this project. There was Billy, whose wife died of bowel cancer, leaving him and their five-year old twins behind, who then pivoted his startup company to detect cancer using breath; James, whose young daughter came through a very rare form of eye cancer; Ludo, whose cancer was diagnosed so late that new lumps were popping up literally every day and who went through gruelling treatment to come out the other side; Paul, who has been living with kidney cancer for twelve years now, and many others. It was truly humbling and also very informative to talk to them.

From these reflections and conversations, I distilled the following approaches that have been really helpful for me in my journey so far.

Gather knowledge and understanding

I am the sort of person who wants to research everything. I am probably a mild hypochondriac to start with. Add to that avid use of the internet, and I am in danger of becoming a 'cyberchondriac'. As mentioned before, I initially made the mistake of starting to look things up before I had any real information. This is dangerous – you can drown in a morass of 'facts' that are frightening but meaningless. When all I knew was that I had a tumour in my brain, I read that it could be brain cancer or a benign tumour or a secondary tumour, or something else altogether. So I stopped googling and only started to research properly again when the cancer and the mutation had been identified, and the treatment had been decided on. My research means I can remain relatively unemotional about the disease and it helps my relationship with the oncologist because we can talk things over. Also, as James told me: "Understanding about the treatments means that you are more able to prepare mentally for them."

It is important to choose your sources carefully. I use books, the NHS website, generic cancer charity websites and charity websites specific to my cancer. When using Google, I try to see whether the organisation running the website seems to be trustworthy. I also check whether what they are saying is replicated or corroborated elsewhere. I look at the date of publication, whether the research is original and who is funding it. Is it a sales site or pure research? It's also important to remember what Paul, who is on a twelve-year cancer journey, put so bluntly to me: "Don't get terrified by the rubbish online. Stats in particular, averages, medians, they are not about you." So I try to keep perspective. I also distinguish between UK and USA sites. Certain treatments may not be available in both countries, or treatments may be done in a different way. If I do find something that appears to be of use, I discuss it with David, my oncologist, and certainly don't just embark on some treatment or drug without his advice. David puts it like this: "There is lots of information out there, but with genetically modified lung cancers we are getting into a form of personalised medicine, so we are zooming in to treatments which are very specific to a patient's particular cancer. What works for one person may not be at all applicable to another."

I find it really encouraging as well as interesting to learn about the latest scientific research. I had a long chat with Kat Arney, author of the fascinating book *Rebel Cell: Cancer, Evolution and the Science of Life* and learned a great deal about current and emerging understanding of the cancer mechanism and potential treatments that are being developed, some of which are not that far into the future. I guess I am in an arms race – staying alive long enough to be there when new treatments come through.

Talk about it

Hopefully we all have some circles of support around us already; first immediate family and close friends, and then people who are less close. For me, immediate family consisted of my adult children and Liesbeth. It was important to me to tell my sons in a way that was not too upsetting. It is disturbing enough to have a cancer diagnosis, but I tried to do it sensitively. Liesbeth has been with me every step of the way, coming to appointments to be a second set of ears and take notes. At the start of my journey, when things were extremely uncertain, I only shared it with very few close friends. It was very worrying for me because I didn't actually have a diagnosis and you don't want to frighten people too much.

For some people, it works best to keep it just in the immediate family. It can be easier for those around you if they don't have to continuously respond to lots of kindly meant enquiries. For me, once I had the diagnosis and the treatment was starting to work, I found it helpful to talk to other people about it and to be quite open. This had many benefits. It meant I was getting emotional support in all sorts of ways: good conversations, practical help, generous gestures. It also enabled me to make something good come out of a bad situation by spreading knowledge and awareness, taking away stigma. I spent less time dwelling on my own situation. As Ludo, who went through gruelling treatment and found himself supporting others on his ward who were worse off, put it: "It helped not to think about myself, but to think about others." And maybe most importantly, it can help save lives. Billy, again: "When someone is diagnosed, other people don't know what to do. My wife was quite firmly of the view: say something, it doesn't have to be perfect, you can't fix the situation with words, but you can just say: I'm here. Acknowledge it. If we can talk about cancer more, it can make it a little bit easier for people with cancer or their families to talk about it and also, more awareness of cancer and gastro-intestinal problems will get more people checked out by a doctor sooner." Once I opened up about my cancer, it transpired that friends knew other people who were able to help with information or experiences that were useful for me. Here it is important to screen carefully, as some information can be inaccurate and some experiences not applicable to you.

Being open also means you establish contact with another set of people, namely fellow sufferers. Their journey is not yours, but you share a lot and you learn for instance how to deal with the professionals, your dedicated oncology team, as it is so important to have a good relationship with them. I have also had a tremendous amount of support from dedicated charities, in my case the Roy Castle Lung Cancer Foundation and EGFR+, the charity for my specific cancer mutation. Billy, whose wife died of cancer: "What initially felt like a very lonely experience – this is happening to me – being able online to see other people going through this, their stories, their journeys, I think helped her."

Carry on with normal life

I find it tremendously helpful to carry on as normal as much as possible. I am fortunate so far that the treatment is working well and I don't suffer from terrible side-effects. But even Ludo, who went through the heaviest possible treatment, says: "Don't let it take over, carry on as much as you can, it stops you getting bored and feeling sorry for yourself." Paul puts it like this: "I don't let the cancer dominate everything I do. The cancer is part of me, it's not all of me."

In my case, this approach was the obvious one for me. My life basically consists of taking sets of problems and solving them – that's what I do and have done for a living. Once I got my head around the diagnosis, after several weeks, I packaged it up as something I've just got to work on – and work on together with the NHS. I like to use every minute of the day and since the minutes are even more precious now than they already were, I make sure to do what I enjoy and want to do, and to shed things I can really do without.

Exercise

I cannot overstate how important it is for me to stay fit. The fitter you are, the better you are able to withstand treatments and to feel good. Ludo is very clear about his own situation. If he hadn't been as fit as he was, they would not have been able to give him the heaviest possible chemo treatment and he might not be here now. Paul, in his interview, said it in his typical direct way: "Eat well and exercise. Don't give up, don't curl into a ball on the couch and watch Netflix all day."

When the treatment had settled down, I went back to running and in fact ran the Cambridge Half Marathon with family and friends just over a year after the diagnosis, this time to raise money for suicide prevention.

Stay positive

This is a tricky one. A cancer diagnosis is frightening, even nowadays when there are so many more treatments available. My personal approach is to be positive but realistic at the same time. Face up to the facts, yes, but do all you can to beat the odds. No one can always be positive, but it helps you to get through treatment. Being positive is clearly also much easier for the people around you.

Ludo: "I had the end game in mind."

Paul: "Stay positive. In the ward after the operation, the doctor said to me: it's the positive patients that get better quickly. Patients who feel sorry for themselves spiral down. We've got to keep almost a bit of self-delusion. Enjoy the time that you have. Every day is a bonus."

Build up a good relationship with your medical team

I use the term 'joint venture' here. I know it's a business term, but I come from the business world. The way I see it, we work together, David the oncologist and me. It's really important to feel that you are in the room with someone who's on your side. Of course it is not just the oncologist; David is supported by a whole team. This consists of more junior doctors and specialist lung cancer nurses, who run a support helpline and email system. I had to find out who they all were and what their roles and responsibilities were. James said: "We used all the phone numbers they gave us."

For oncologist appointments, I bring a list of symptoms and questions and if I've found some research which I think might be of interest, I bring it along too. On one occasion, David suggested I might want to consider a drug that would help rebuild my bone. He explained the pros and cons and then I went away to look into it. The next time we met, I had some more information and had had time to weigh it up. We had a fruitful discussion and decided that I wasn't going to start it, at least not at that time. It is vital for me to have a good working relationship with the team, and that includes from time to time, when appropriate, being able to challenge them. But there is absolutely no place for anger. The emotion is all on the patient's side and to remain calm is so critical.

Keep as much control as you can

It is much easier to manage emotions, to remain calm, to undergo treatment and not let the cancer dominate your life if you feel a degree of control. In simple ways, for me, that means doing all the things already mentioned so far that I can do myself and that are going to help me live as long as possible: to be in the long tail of the bell curve of survival. Be healthy, be positive, understand what is happening, ask for support when appropriate. But it also applies more directly to interactions with my medical team. As mentioned before, I take an agenda to consultations, with questions and queries, and I try to work with the NHS to have my appointments at times that suit my other activities in life. I am lucky enough to be in a position to buy in certain treatments and I use that capacity to make treatments fit in with my life. It was interesting to hear how this sense of control applied even in the case of James' very young daughter. The medical staff made sure she was part of what was happening to her – for instance, by letting her hold her own t-shirt in the right place to have a procedure carried out.

Plan and prepare

There was huge stress in the period leading up to the definite diagnosis and treatment. I wasn't sleeping, I was wondering whether I was going to die in a month or less, and I couldn't plan anything. The lack of sleep was partly due to the steroids I was on. I spent hours in the night trying to set my affairs in order, as they say, rewriting my will and organising my quite complicated financial affairs as an early-stage investor in such a way that if I were to die someone could pick up the pieces. Paul says: "Prepare for the fact that you could die. Make any preparations, don't leave it till the last minute. I wrote seven personal letters for each of my children to open one each year for seven years after I die. Think what you need to do, make sure it isn't hanging over you at the end."

Once we had the diagnosis and treatment had started, it was still difficult to plan anything. I wasn't particularly well and we had to wait and see how the treatment bedded in, whether I was going to have side effects that might require hospitalisation. Luckily, the treatment started to work and I began to feel a lot better. As described earlier, for me it was important to go and see relatives and close friends around the country and also to spend quality one-on-one time with my sons – that helped me a lot. Once the treatment settled down and I was on a three-monthly scan schedule, Liesbeth and I started living in three-month-instalments. We simply planned from scan to scan. If the scan results were positive, that was the green light for us to plan the next three months. The longer this went on, the less stressful it became and the more we started to think beyond just three months. My way of living became one of hope, due to successful treatment which allowed me to live a more-or-less normal life, with just a whiff of denial thrown in for good measure.

My 500-day plan

There are and have been hundreds of thousands of people with my type of cancer, so there are studies. In some cases these studies cover hundreds of participants, which means a lot of data. Statistically with my mutation and Stage IVB, according to one study, the average period from the start of treatment to the first mutation is 18.6 months. Of course I hoped to be in the lucky half, the 50% of patients who have a period longer than 18.6 months before their cancer mutates, but it wasn't meant to be. My cancer mutated after 17.9 months, as will be detailed later on. So I looked at the data again, and the average time from mutation to death is around eighteen months, which is about 500 days, so in my almost over-logical way I have been working on a 500-day plan, with my life coach Katy.

When I tell this to people, they sometimes give me a strange look. Apart from in novels such as *The Immortalists*, no one knows when they will die. That knowledge could be looked upon as being supremely worrying or perhaps powerful or even comforting.

I am hoping of course that I will live another 5,000 days (to beyond eighty) but I have things to do – this book is a great example – things to close down (formal board roles), things to document (I still haven't finished putting my affairs in order) and time to spend with Liesbeth, Matt and several close friends, before I expect to be less able to enjoy myself because I will be having regular chemo- or immunotherapy infusions at Addenbrooke's Hospital.

The 500-day plan is a 'living document': I am tweaking it every fifty days to tick off the things I have done, and fleshing out the experiences I want to share with others.

But of course, 50% of the mutated cancer sufferers will die before the eighteen months, so I must not be complacent. This seems the most intense part of my life as I now have a statistically derived time before I die (accurate to within a few months of my death), a very unusual 'target' for any human being. To some extent I need to start grieving for my own passing, to try and ensure I have an orderly end, to hug and say goodbye to many people. Yet with medical help and outright luck, I may last many more years. From what others say and how they behave towards me, I don't seem to be showing my internal unease and my mental and physical health are both still in a very good state.

This may seem cold and emotionless, but I feel I am planning my last months alive in the same way that I operated as an entrepreneur: spreadsheets, actions, timing, documents. I have been told that I am lucky to be able to plan in this fashion. Everyone will have their own way of dealing with a diagnosis like mine, but I feel comforted that I have a level of control of my final months and years.

Chapter 18
Alan

Just as I felt I was getting a grip on living with cancer, my life was turned upside down yet again.

I knew when we started writing this book that this would be the most difficult piece of text that I would ever write. I had said at Ian's life celebration in Cambridge that reading out his eulogy would be the most difficult thing I would ever have to do. I was too grief-stricken to even speak the words I wrote for Alan's eulogy at his funeral.

As I write this, about a year after Alan's death, there are many people who knew and loved him who are still deeply grieving. I hope that no one is affected by what I am writing here, but for clearly tragic reasons, Alan's death is a huge part of what I am now, so it needs a place in this book. Alan died by suicide on the 23rd of October 2022.

I will not go into any detail about exactly what happened or may have happened, other than to say there was no doubt that he took his own life.

Instead, I will talk about how I coped, how I grieved, and where my heart and mind lie now. You may speculate what led to Alan taking his own life. The coroner reached a conclusion based on evidence she gathered, but I worked through for myself what we could or perhaps should have done, and I know others around him did the same. In time I created my own narrative of why he took his life, which is an important part of my coping strategy for getting 'through' the tragedy of losing him and being able to continue with life.

* * * * *

Liesbeth and I had flown to South America on the 15th of October 2022. Friends of ours had been to Ecuador and the Galapagos Islands earlier in the year and raved about it and so we had put together a six-week trip.

I had seen Alan two days before we flew to Quito and had been chatting to him via WhatsApp over the next ten days. He told me that for a bit of fun and pocket money, he had grown his hair so he could be an extra in the Leonard Bernstein biographical film, *Maestro*. The scene was set in Ely Cathedral, recreating the time when Bernstein had conducted the London Symphony Orchestra there in the early 1970s. Alan's role was to be a member of the audience. Late on the 23rd of October, I WhatsApp-chatted to him about family things such as our upcoming trip at Christmas and his brother Ian's visit to the Atacama desert many years before, where Liesbeth and I were headed after Ecuador.

The next morning, the 24th of October, we were heading down from the Ecuadorian capital of Quito to the Avenue of Volcanoes, in a car with a driver and guide, when I received a WhatsApp message from Paul, who manages Martlet Capital, where Alan worked.

The message said:

> *Hope you are having a wonderful time.*
> *Sorry to ask but we have not heard from Alan all day as he hasn't shown up for work – can you drop Tasha a text/ WhatsApp as we are understandably concerned for him.*

This was about 10:30am our time in Ecuador and mid-afternoon in the UK. The next few hours were indescribably awful. Only a few people know some of what happened, and it would do much more harm than good to share further.

We'd parked at the entrance of the Cotopaxi National Park, and after increasingly frantic feelings of concern and helplessness, I heard on a phone call that Alan was dead and I collapsed onto the cold wet tarmac, where Liesbeth and I clung on to each other.

Our guide Mauricio had heard my side of the traumatic telephone calls leading up to this moment. Liesbeth explained to him what had happened and that we had to get back to the UK as soon as possible. As we were driven back into Quito, he rang his local contacts and we were booked onto the next KLM flight back to London via Amsterdam. We said goodbye to Mauricio and boarded. The crew had been told the circumstances and we were put in an area of business class that they had cleared for us.

We made phone calls from the airports we were routed through and once back at Heathrow, Matt collected us from the airport and we drove on to Tasha at her and Alan's home.

Later that night, I sent this text to a very close friend:

The awful thing about this terrible terrible tragedy is that I've had the "dress rehearsal" with Ian. I know the emotional roller coaster. I know the way my mind is protecting me – for instance I can look at photos of Alan (with great pain and tears) but can't bring his face to mind. I know the police and coroner and funeral and inquest process. I know how much love and support (and helplessness) is around me and Tasha and Matt from family, friends of mine and friends of Alan. I know the pain I and everyone who knew him are enduring will ease over the months and years. I have the fucking T-shirt. I am so so sad, but I'm a survivor and I will continue helping and loving other people and absorbing their love and support. This has been so hard but cathartic to type. Thanks for being a dear friend x

The following month was a blur as we organised Alan's funeral and I began to piece together his last few weeks. As we should have been in South America for another five weeks, our diaries were completely empty.

A fortnight after his death, it was Alan's birthday, and Tasha decided to go ahead with running a local half marathon, together with many of her and Alan's friends. It was going to be an impossibly hard day and this way, Tasha gave his friends a focus, something to do to remember Alan by. She and Alan had planned this event together and wanted to raise money for a charity. So now I put together a charitable giving page for Alan himself hoping to raise £10,000 for suicide prevention charities. Over the next few months, we raised £60,000.

One of my coping mechanisms was to busy myself in investigating which were the most relevant charities locally, nationally and internationally. With the help of friends, I contacted several mental health and suicide prevention charities, and one of the first things I learnt was that suicide is the most common cause of death for males between twenty and forty years old. Coincidentally, I was also introduced via my physiotherapist to the International Association for Suicide Prevention.

In cafés and on walks, I shed many tears with close friends, including Alison, who thought of Alan as a son. I found a bereavement counsellor whom I saw a few times, which helped, although he said several times that he thought he may be "too zen" for me. Of course Liesbeth and I talked a lot about Alan and what had happened. Friends travelled to see me from their homes around the country and they opened up about their own dark times. For instance, a friend told me he had tried to take his own life whilst at university – I thought I knew him very well, but we all keep secrets even from our closest friends – partly perhaps as we are ashamed, partly as we don't want to revisit and partly due to the stigma associated with suicide and mental health in the UK.

It was the schools' half-term holiday and neither Tasha nor Matt, who both worked at the same school, went back to work that term. This was both expected and welcomed by their employer.

Matt and I decided to have some time together and as it was too early in the season to ski and my hiking ability was still poor after my plantar fasciitis, we decided to hire a yacht for a few days. That was such a special time for me – one-to-one talking, eating, sharing the sailing, although it was mostly me at the wheel and Matt scampering around the boat. We were lucky with the weather and circumnavigated the Bay of Naples.

I knew that I needed to see Alan, to say goodbye. I have never regretted not seeing Ian after he died, but knew I might do, if I didn't see Alan. I knew I would need deep inner strength and that it would be extremely upsetting, but I am very glad that I did see him. Liesbeth came with me and we entered the room together – an indication of the strength of our relationship.

If Alan had been experiencing deep mental turmoil, it gave me some comfort to believe he was now at peace. But this comfort is limited; I continue to break down when I drive or cycle past the funeral home.

The funeral was held in a crematorium south of Cambridge, a beautiful spot on a hill near where he and Tasha lived. It was a large room but was so full that many people had to stand in the entrance or outside. Remembering the occasion wracks me with grief, not just for his widow and his brother but for his many friends and colleagues. We had a wake nearby and Liesbeth took the microphone, describing how warm Alan was when she first met him, and inviting others to share their memories of him, too.

I knew that the flow of adrenaline that keeps one going after a close death suddenly ceases after the funeral and that this can be an emotional crash, so Liesbeth and I had booked a small cottage in the Yorkshire Dales to go to straight after the funeral. It had an open fire and room for Matt if he wanted to join us and it was close to two friends whom I had known for nearly fifty years. We rested, strolled, read, talked and started to replan our life.

Christmas was still a month away and we wanted to restart our South American trip. I knew that doing this would help me to be distracted through travelling and being away from England, but I needed a clear set of scans first.

We also decided not to cancel family events. We felt it was better to carry on as normal and of course, it helped with keeping busy and was a good distraction, although any family event will always be especially sad when members of the family are absent through death. In this period, I also attended the funeral of a friend from university who died from cancer, the person who had introduced me to the concept of the 'fuck-it' list.

Dawn and Giles visited us in Cambridge from New Zealand. They'd been unable to make the funeral a month earlier, although Dawn had sent in a wonderful tribute and the link to one of Alan's favourite New Zealand songs, which we played at the funeral. It was so good to spend time with them as Dawn had been very close to Alan.

I realised that for my own sanity, and because I was terminally ill, I could not spend several years working out my narrative of how and why Alan had died. With Ian, I had found that this narrative evolved as more information became available. I knew that for me, grieving enters a new phase once I am satisfied that I know as much as I ever will, so I needed to do the same in the case of Alan.

With Alan the situation was clearer than with Ian. The coroner's preliminary inquest report was available within six weeks, and we were offered a hearing in early January (which, in the event, we postponed). In the case of Ian, I never saw the inquest report, but that was thirteen years earlier and of course procedures have changed. Naturally some of the report on Alan's death was redacted. There were images and contact email addresses that it would have been wrong for the family to see. Sixteen people had provided information, although over half were members of the emergency services who were present when Alan was found.

Although he was my son, he was a thirty-four-year-old adult and so there were many aspects of his life I could not possibly have been expected to know about. This meant that there was information in the report that really shocked me and caused me to significantly alter the narrative I had developed up to that point.

Although I am embarrassed to say this, I needed to know more about exactly how it happened than I felt was normal. It felt morbid to read some sections of the report. But it was helpful to meet the most senior police officer on the case and she was able to add some more detail to her section of the inquest report. She also said that she had enough evidence by the evening after Alan's death to conclude it was no longer a police matter and hence she handed the case over promptly to the coroner.

The final piece of the narrative jigsaw was the inquest hearing itself. This happened after Liesbeth and I had returned from South America the second time and had travelled to Australia, in April, so I joined by video link. I sincerely hope this is the last inquest I ever attend, and to the relief of everyone concerned, there were no press or public in the room.

The coroner's finding is nowadays called a conclusion – it was known as a 'verdict' until 2013, when coronial law was overhauled, putting the bereaved at the centre of the process and emphasising the 'finding of fact'. The conclusion is not a public document unless the press is present and publish it. In the case of Alan, the coroner had written what is called a narrative conclusion, which is defined as a brief explanation of the facts of how the person came by their death. She didn't mention suicide. This conclusion caused me some consternation, as it seemed to leave other possibilities open.

However, my concerns were soon alleviated. I had got to know the chief executive of the UK-based PAPYRUS Prevention of Young Suicide charity (to which a donation is made from every sale of this book), called Ged Flynn. Through sharing his knowledge and by connecting me with a senior coroner, I learnt a lot more about the whole process.

The conclusion was not 'open' as with Ian, and I understand that the coroner would have needed to have read a note from Alan or seen other evidence that he had intended to take his life before she could have arrived at the short-form conclusion of 'suicide'.

Once I had thought this through again, my narrative became fixed. I knew all I needed to know about the 'how' and, with the help of others, I had thought through enough about the 'why'.

This did not mean I was any less sad about his tragic death, but it meant I could concentrate fully on staying healthy, on loving Liesbeth and Matt, and contributing to my and other people's lives as much as I could.

As with any grief, there are triggers, many triggers, and writing this has been even worse than I expected. A close friend, Anne, produced a lino print of Alan's beaming and bearded face, which she framed and which now sits above my desk, to watch over me and remind me. A photo of Ian is to my left, together with a cloth printed with a piece from the Dalai Lama titled 'NEVER GIVE UP', which Ian had given me. A photo of all three boys and me taken in 1999 sits behind me.

Chapter 19
Life with Cancer

In the period before the inquest hearing, the Christmas period of 2022, we made plans to have as much of the family together as possible, thinking it might be my last Christmas, but also the first Christmas without Alan. We booked a large apartment in Funchal, the capital of Madeira, which is far enough south to be warm in mid-winter. Liesbeth and I were joined by Matt and his girlfriend, as well as Liesbeth's two daughters plus one boyfriend. We hiked and walked along the levadas and tried canyoning, a first for all of us except Matt. This is where, in a wetsuit, helmeted and with a guide, you make your way down a fairly steep river, abseiling down waterfalls, jumping and swimming in pools, sliding down rocks and more. We hadn't laughed so much in ages.

My foot was still recovering from plantar fasciitis, and I struggled with the longer walks, especially downhill. On New Year's Eve, close friend Richard joined us with his partner and her daughter – the fireworks around the city are famous around the world.

As mentioned above, in January Liesbeth and I headed back to Ecuador, avoiding the section where we had heard about Alan's death and heading to the Galapagos for possibly the best week in my many experiences of travelling to nearly ninety countries.

The animals on the Galapagos Islands have had no predators for thousands of years of evolution, so they show no fear in the presence of humans or other animals. British and other countries' whalers in the mid-19th century had taken a terrible toll of animals on these islands, but the Ecuadorian government, with help from the rest of the world, has since spent decades ensuring they and their extraordinary and fragile environment are protected.

This meant that when we landed on a remote island, the iguanas, the seals and even an albatross completely ignored us. Darwin wrote *On the Origin of the Species* based on his research on the islands in the 1830s and it was astonishing to see the finches and giant tortoises that had developed differently even if only a few tens of miles apart on different islands.

In the autumn of 2022, before Alan's death, Liesbeth and I had discussed getting married, and Liesbeth's attitude was so supportive and loving – I had terminal cancer, although obviously hoping to survive for another two decades if medical advances kept ahead of me. She said she had one request: she wanted "to be proposed to properly."

We'd chosen an engagement ring together in Cambridge before we left on our trip, and I had this in my hand luggage. Of course I felt it would be much safer on her finger. But where could I propose in a romantic location, especially as we were not allowed to leave the small cruise ship (eighteen passengers) without a crew member? I secretly mentioned this to one of the wonderful Galapagoan guides. In her twenty years showing people around the islands, she had witnessed two marriages but never an engagement, and was pleased to accept the challenge. A few days later I was asked to ensure that Liesbeth and I were on a two-man kayak, that I had the ring and that I steered the kayak towards the beach.

I sat in the rear and Liesbeth, in the front, was very confused. She didn't understand why we were heading to the beach when we were meant to be looking at the fish and sea life in the water below us. The guide joined us on the beach and invited us to climb up to a lookout platform. Liesbeth started to well up as she began to realise what was happening. When we reached the platform, the boat crew had set up a table with paper flowers,

non-alcoholic fizz and a banner with 'Will You Marry Me'
printed on it. By this time, we were both in floods of tears.
So many emotions came out: around Alan's death, around the
two of us growing closer and the unbelievably romantic setting.
In my confusion, I dropped to the wrong knee (probably as I
wasn't wearing my sword). The weather and views were simply
perfect and Liesbeth said yes!

The other passengers, in boats and kayaks scattered on the
sea below us, were told via the walkie-talkie and cheers erupted
into the blue sky. That evening a party for all the passengers and
crew was held and during the karaoke Liesbeth sang a beautiful
rendition of 'Blue Moon'.

With the guide's help, I had managed to create the romantic
occasion that Liesbeth (and I) had wanted. We invited everyone
on the boat to the as yet unplanned wedding and two of them
actually joined us a few months later.

We then went on to have an amazing time in Peru, Chile
and Argentina, including visiting the island of Cape Horn – not
many people achieve that due to the stormy weather.

We returned home to a cool winter and began to prepare
for our next trip and for our wedding. We visited the PAPYRUS
suicide prevention charity, for which we had raised £30,000 after
Alan's death, and the Roy Castle Lung Cancer foundation – the
largest UK charity for lung cancer sufferers.

Maggi, a friend who I had known since my Stamford days,
and who had flown from the USA for Alan's funeral, joined us to
run the Cambridge Half Marathon, where a group of us raised
money for a Cambridgeshire local young person's mental health
charity, Centre33. It was the first half marathon for Liesbeth and
Maggi, and I was forty minutes slower than when I ran the same
route just before my cancer was detected. But I was still there
and still running.

Liesbeth and I had been skiing just before Christmas in
France and I had a second ski trip of the season with friends,

Paul, Geoff and Cornelia. My skiing ability was not as good as before Covid, not due to my balance, which was back to normal, but because I had not regained my fitness.

The next six-week trip Liesbeth and I made was self-organised and mainly focused on spending time with family and friends. We flew via Hong Kong to New Zealand where we first explored the most northerly parts in a campervan, then had a lovely Easter weekend with Dawn and Giles. We visited haunts of Ian and Alan, who had both loved living in New Zealand, spreading more ashes.

We then flew down to the South Island and joined Maggi to walk the Abel Tasman Trail and then explored North Island, again in a campervan, where we hiked the Tongariro Crossing. This effectively means walking a half marathon with an 800m height gain and loss through stunning volcanic landscape. I was close to my limit at the end of this. We did a couple of Parkruns in Auckland before heading to Melbourne to spend time with Susie, my brother's widow, and with my co-director at Camdata in the 1980s. Alan's inquest hearing was scheduled for when we were in Australia, so we attended that by video link, as described previously.

After spending a week driving up to Sydney to see some of my Australian cousins, I met up with my first employer, Dick Smith, who, having started with one electronics shop in 1974, had gone on to become probably Australia's most famous entrepreneur and explorer. We spent three hours reminiscing, then it was time for a concert at the Sydney Opera House before flying to Japan the next day, where we spent a further week.

Shortly after I returned I was awarded a Lifetime Achievement Award by the *Cambridge Independent*, a local newspaper, where I gave a ten-minute talk about what I had learned over the decades.

Liesbeth moved in with me and over the following weeks the house became our home. Matt moved out to be the second lodger with Tasha, convenient and companiable for both of them, although it was an hour's cycle for Matt into his work at the school. Matt and I went hiking and saw each other two or three times a month, except over the summer, when he cycled to and from Switzerland, where he still has many friends, having lived there for about a decade.

I continued to unwind from roles and once my cancer had mutated, I started working on my eighteen-month plan, as mentioned earlier. They say that we all have a book in us, and I had already published two with the help of a professional author, but these were business-related books and covered little of my life. Having talked to Liesbeth and Katy, in the summer I wrote a couple of thousand words about Ian's death, to see what it felt like to document deeply personal experiences and thoughts, and then decided that I would write this, with Liesbeth's help.

Whilst in New Zealand, I had been offered an honorary doctorate by Anglia Ruskin University, the 'other' university in Cambridge, which has a large campus in that city, but is also present in four other locations. It was the *Times Higher Education* University of the Year 2023. I was honoured to accept and receive the award, a Doctor of Business Administration, at the Corn Exchange in Cambridge in July. I made an acceptance speech to the hundreds of graduands and their families, starting by mentioning my previous connection to ARU being Alan's first-class Economics degree from that university.

Liesbeth and I got married on the 24th of June 2023, and it was a joyous celebration, despite missing Alan and Ian, and the cloud of the cancer hanging over us. Maybe the cloud of cancer actually made it more joyous – we were enjoying everything we possibly could.

The week before, some local friends, with Liesbeth's help, had organised a surprise stag do for me. It was a complete shock when I walked out of the house to see the group of friends in a taxi! A dozen of us had a guided foraging event in local woods, enjoyed a fine meal and then two games of croquet at the Jockey Club in Newmarket.

The day itself started with a private ceremony with family and close friends Sue and Pete, followed in the evening by a ceilidh with one hundred family and friends in a hotel on the banks of the River Cam, including an American couple who had been on the cruise with us in the Galapagos and who were travelling the world. The weather was fabulous and the day couldn't have gone better. Sunday was reserved for the thirty or so people who had travelled from abroad, with a punting-and-picnic trip up the river to Grantchester Meadows and a barbecue at home.

Then, almost exactly eighteen months after diagnosis, the dreaded day arrived where my three-monthly scans showed one of the tumours, located in the pelvis, had started to mutate and was being 'active'. It was growing. A PET scan a few days later showed that it was only that tumour; none of the others was active. We discussed the options in a consultation with the oncologist, who recommended treating that tumour specifically with radiotherapy, after carrying out a bone biopsy to determine the genetic mutation that had taken place in that tumour. He explained that there were two forms of radiotherapy. One is a type called stereotactic radiotherapy, or stereotactic ablative body radiotherapy (SABR), trade names of which can include Cyberknife, which is a state-of-the-art, highly focused method. The other is conventional radiotherapy, which is still very effective, though maybe slightly less so than the newer type. He put my case to the commissioning committee of my hospital, Addenbrooke's in Cambridge, to get approval to give me the SABR treatment, as I seemed to meet all criteria. Unfortunately I was turned down because the tumour was what is called synchronous. This means it was already there at initial diagnosis, and had simply started to grow. To qualify for SABR under NICE guidelines, your tumour has to be metachronous – that is to say, it has to be new.

My options now were to accept the conventional radiotherapy, two times five consecutive days of radiation at Addenbrooke's, with a weekend in the middle, or to pay for SABR myself and have it done privately in the town of Newmarket, not far from Cambridge, where my oncologist also works. This would mean just three sessions, with a day in between each time. To complicate matters, Liesbeth and I had booked a holiday in Iceland with her two daughters, which we had jokingly called our 'honeymoon', and which was all paid for and ready to go. Talking to David the oncologist about it, we decided that it would take time to get me ready for the treatment anyway, so that we could, if we wanted to, do all the preparatory scans and tests beforehand, then go away for our twelve-day trip and get the treatment immediately upon our return. So this is what we decided. I was so lucky to be able to have the choice. The treatment is not cheap, but it meant that I received the very best option, with the added bonus that it took a lot less time out of my life, because it was only three sessions and I could choose times and days to suit me. I kept a lot of control over my life and didn't have to cancel the holiday. To my mind, that was all absolutely worth it.

The treatment went well and didn't cause many side-effects for me other than some skin burn. I managed to fit the three radiotherapy sessions around a trip to educate angel investors in Dublin and then hiking on the west coast of Ireland with friend Richard. The pain in the tumour site in my pelvis, which had been getting steadily worse even as we were in Iceland, almost immediately started to reduce, which was great news. I had been warned about various side effects, but the only one that affected me was mild pelvic pain (other than from the tumour) which meant I could not run my usual 5km a few times a week. My oncologist said that this was not something that concerned most of his patients!

I had also been told that I was likely to start noticing for myself whether the radiation had worked long before the medics could see any change on the scans, and this appeared to be the case. Liesbeth and I were therefore able to visit her brother and sister-in-law in the Dordogne in France and I attended a conference in Slovenia on suicide prevention later that summer.

Following my 500-day plan, which was now down to about 350 days, I had resigned from other roles, finally finishing with Martlet on my 68th birthday, twelve years after I had co-founded the organisation. I was transitioning so that much more of my time was spent on my bucket list and very little on my fuck-it list. I also bought a ten-year-old open-top Porsche 911, something I could have afforded for several years, but not been able to justify until I was terminally ill.

We'd planned to visit Africa for a month in September but abandoned that once the cancer mutated. But the scans in September were clear, so Liesbeth managed to create a fabulous twelve-day trip to Zimbabwe and Botswana at a week's notice. There was some risk involved in being in a remote part of the Okavango Delta in Botswana where the only method of transport is a small passenger plane. We had travel insurance, which had paid out after we returned home suddenly on Alan's death, but I wondered whether they would pay if I needed urgent medical care. I have always been comfortable with analysing risk as all people, but especially entrepreneurs, have to be.

I have started being more open about life, on my own and other people's podcasts, and recorded several where I talked about how I have coped and learnt from the tragedies in my life.

Although I am not looking forward to my last days and weeks when my health and quality of living may be very poor, I believe I will accept death when it comes. I may even have an alcoholic drink in my last few days. My biggest regret will be the grieving that family and friends will endure, especially Matt.

Chapter 20
Reflections

The majority of this book, like any memoir, covers my life from birth, but here I am adding some thoughts, analysing and reflecting on my life.

Self-reflection seems quite difficult for me because extroverts (which I believe I am) prefer working with others and bouncing ideas back and forth. I have done some of that with family and friends, but Liesbeth and I have also spent tens of hours writing this chapter.

This reflection process is continuously developing, as I speak to family, friends, colleagues and in interviews for the media and for podcasts. Hence, this chapter is a living document. A longer version, including many facts and numbers that give an overview of my life, is on the book's website, which I will occasionally update until I die. There, you can read how many cars and houses I have owned, how many times I've been to court, why I no longer play eighteen-hole golf and many other tidbits of information.

Liesbeth asked me during courting what nourishes my soul. This took some analysis and, although perhaps a little unconventional, I eventually replied "numbers and people." I find comfort in numbers, storing and analysing them. I need to spend time with people, although with sufficient intellectual stimulation or when running, hiking or skiing, I can happily spend hours by myself. Below, I will try to put into words some of the larger and smaller things I've discovered about myself and about life in my sixty-eight years to date.

Some general reflections

I generally have good health. I've only spent three nights in hospital in my life and although I was overweight for many years, have been lucky in that it hasn't affected my physical health as much as it could have done. My alcoholism hasn't led to long-term problems, unless it made me more susceptible to the lung cancer that I now have. Despite leading an active lifestyle with running, hiking, skiing and real tennis, I haven't slept that well since I've got sober. I have learnt that analysing a mathematical problem helps me sleep. For instance: 'what percentage of the world's power output would be needed to pull the Moon closer to the earth by one metre per year?' and 'if one drops a football into the Atlantic Ocean, what height is the ripple on the other side?' I'm happy with my active lifestyle and don't miss alcohol, especially now that non-alcoholic drinks are so much more interesting than they used to be.

My mental health, whilst generally strong, has had its ups and downs. There was a very bad patch for several years towards the end of my first marriage and the end of my drinking. For example, I remember walking our Labrador in a local wood and being absolutely convinced I was being followed. I am glad that I accepted short-term prescribed medication and discovered the benefits of longer-term therapy and counselling. On diagnosis of my cancer, I went through a very difficult patch for about three months. It's not easy to stare one's imminent mortality in the face. But once the osimertinib tablets started to work, I soon reverted to my old self, with a positive outlook on life. This was very different from the sudden tragedies in my life, such as losing Ian and Alan. Those episodes plunged me into deep grief, which to some extent will be with me forever, but that is a 'normal' and 'healthy' response, and in my case didn't affect my mental health.

I have discovered that I like to plan my time carefully, and although I understand the adage 'it is better to be on time, than in time', I would rather be on time. For instance, I am somewhat obsessed with being in the optimum seat on a plane or carriage on a train to exit the airport or station quickly.

However, I would not go as far as Ingvar Kamprad, the founder of IKEA, who once said: 'Time is your most important resource. You can do so much in ten minutes. Ten minutes, once gone, are gone for good. Divide your life into ten-minute units and sacrifice as few of them as possible in meaningless activities.'

On the other hand, I don't like regular weekly routines. Of course, I have had fixed weekly educational courses or badminton or bridge with others, where I try to adhere to those commitments, but I have found that I thrive on a slightly chaotic diary, packing weekdays (and many weekends) with activities. Perhaps this is part of my need to keep busy as a coping mechanism, perhaps combined with the need for constant stimulation and the need to not be 'boxed in'.

I have discovered that I have little interest in and appreciation of music, art and literature, but I do like theatre and cinema, because I think I need a (preferably quite fast-moving) storyline to engage with a performance. As to literature, I wish I was more of a book reader, because I feel I'm missing out on a huge range of learning, entertainment and relaxation. For me, reading books is something that requires prioritisation and I read less than ten books per year.

Although I initially adopted my parents' conservative politics, I was later influenced by my aunt in Australia, friends and exposure to charities into moving more to left of centre, and my natural political position is somewhere between Liberal Democrat and Labour.

This isn't really a reflection, since I've known this from early childhood, but I love technology. I have been an early adopter all my life, getting my first cellular phone in 1985 and buying one of the first shipment of hybrid Audis into the UK.

I have found that I am curious to the point of nosiness. I love learning, whether structured or unstructured, which is probably to do with that need for intellectual stimulation. For many years, my WhatsApp status has been 'Strong opinions, weakly held'. This is a quote that was first attributed to Bob Johansen at the Palo Alto Institute for the Future. I've adopted this because I wanted to build my personal brand and so needed strong public opinions, but it is important to me that they are not set in stone. I find that I like listening to and learning from everyone I meet and will happily alter my views and share the fact that I have done so.

I find thinking about my own character quite hard – I wouldn't want to analyse myself. Instead I will quote from friend Phil, who said something that felt true:

"I always think of Peter as a pragmatic genius, if a little 'Rain Man' around the edges, someone who could cut through the bullshit, and get to the nub of any situation or issue quicker than most. I think this pragmatism is reflected in his approach to his health and potentially his eventual death."

I have discovered that I enjoy working for charities, offering time rather than money. I joined my first charitable board for experience, and soon realised I had business skills and experience to offer and hence helped charities for the following fifteen years, which has given me great satisfaction.

Money

What, on reflection, do I feel about money? I think I have always 'worked' hard, by which I mean long hours, partly as I have enjoyed what I do, partly as I struggle to say no and partly as escapism from other parts of life. I put 'work' in inverted commas as I have probably spent as much time helping others voluntarily, as being paid to deliver something to a customer or employer. I have earned well, although less than if I had worked in the City of London or managed to climb a corporate ladder. But I've discovered that, apart from cars and a reasonably sized house, great experiences are so much more important to me than assets. I am not a collector of anything material, I don't care about physical appearance, and I don't really care about how much money is in the bank per se, other than as a means to have those great experiences. I find my fulfilment and security in personal relationships, in contributing to others and enjoying my life.

Friends

I have discovered that I am generally pretty open about my life and this often leads to friends being open about theirs. By me helping others, many people have helped me and I have asked for and been given emotional help very many times over the decades. I suspect that I show my vulnerabilities earlier in a developing relationship than others. I have also heard distinctions between real friends and 'deal' friends. My conclusion is that we all have our own definition of what is a friend or a close friend. One definition I have heard is that a close friend is one who you would give money to if they were in a difficult situation, but to my cost, I have found that it is wrong to lend money to friends. A colleague and friend once asked to borrow several thousand pounds. I was happy to lend the money to him and we had a witnessed loan agreement. But in the end, he repaid only £50 and then cut off contact. In hindsight, I should have just given him the money.

Grief

Observing others, I have realised that every person has a different grief journey. Some of the differences are due to the nature of the relationship, any dependency (work, personal, financial), the age and reason for a death, the frequency of recent communication, or how closely one identifies with the person – age, sex, occupation, or fitness.

Over the years, friends have asked and/or observed how I coped. In no particular order in terms of time or priority, I would say that first of all, I have not let grief either overwhelm or define me. Then, I have asked for and been open to help from family, friends and professionals and have very rarely been worried about showing my grief amongst family and friends, or in public. In the process, I hope that I have rarely been selfish in my grieving – I remember only two occasions when I suddenly left a meal or party without telling anyone where I was going, simply to have space.

Another coping mechanism has been researching grieving and trying to work out what techniques applied to me. I think I have only created one ritual: that of spreading Ian/Nam's ashes around the world, and latterly of spreading a mix of his and Alan's ashes.

I have busied myself with life, both as a distraction mechanism and as a way of feeling I am contributing to others, to feel that the loss was channelled into something positive – that 'something good has come out of it'. This has given me a sense of purpose, a reason to get up in the mornings and has contributed strongly to my sense of identity.

I have spent a lot of effort in understanding how I cope with rejection, from a potential customer buying from a competitor instead of me, to a girlfriend breaking off a relationship, to the ultimate, when a child rejected my love and support. I have become more accepting of rejection as I matured, although where the bond is emotional, I am still as hurt as I was in my twenties.

I have been told I am stoic and separately that I am resilient, and I am sure that those are both to some extent true. But I feel that being resilient is emotionally demanding and whilst writing this book, I heard about the concept of post-traumatic growth. I have come to like that description better than stoicism and resilience.

At a recent conference of the International Association of Suicide Prevention (IASP), I learnt of both that term, post-traumatic growth and another term: postvention.

From their website:

> *The International Association for Suicide Prevention is dedicated to preventing suicide and suicidal behaviour and to alleviating its effects. IASP leads the global role in suicide prevention by strategically developing an effective forum that is proactive in creating strong collaborative partnerships and promoting evidence-based action in order to reduce the incidence of suicide and suicidal behaviour.*

I stumbled – very fortunately (my higher power?) – across the organisation because I had a physiotherapy session shortly after Alan died, and a relative of the physiotherapist works for the IASP.

Postvention refers to the actions for the bereaved in response to a suicide. One of IASP's roles is to promote research and best practice in postvention.

Post-traumatic growth (the opposite is post-traumatic depreciation) appears to be what I have experienced. Although I can't tell you how I achieved that growth, I have developed in such a way to handle my grief and to change my behaviour to positively help others.

Is this how I have avoided PTSD?

Looking back

Have I used my sixty-eight years on this earth efficiently? Who am I to answer that question? You will have read about my lost decade, but I do feel I have now caught up. As Jim, the CEO of one of my exited investments said:

"To paraphrase Tyrell in *Blade Runner*: 'The light that burns twice as bright burns half as long' – and you have burned so very, very brightly, Peter."

I am not sure if my risk appetite has increased over time, although I know my ability to analyse and measure risk has improved immeasurably. Whilst being an entrepreneur I have not risked money so much as risked 'opportunity cost' – that is, what could I have done that would have been a better use of my time? I have long been comfortable that I can't change the past. I analysed the risks as much as I could do at the time, and hence feel that I have always made the 'right' decision.

This determination to leave the past in the past also applies in personal life. Ian and Alan are gone. I can't change that. I miss them every day, but I can remember them with love and thankfulness, I can try to help others not having to go through what I went through, and I can try to make the most of the life that is left to me.

Death
And finally, my feelings about my own death. Like anyone of my age, I have been to many funerals, and the most difficult are of those who have died young. Most of those young deaths were due to cancer or an accident, except in the cases of Ian and Alan.

As you have probably deduced, I do like to be in control of my life, I hope not to the extent that it upsets others – although I am sure I have – and I really hope that I can be in control of my death. I have been a supporter of assisted dying for many years. After experiencing my mother's final two years, I am confident that in due course, UK society will introduce procedures such as have been developed in Switzerland, the Netherlands and Canada, although unfortunately this probably won't happen in time for me.

A letter to my nineteen-year-old self
A few years ago, I wrote *A letter to my younger CEO Self* for Shirin Dehghan, an entrepreneur and investor whom I respect immensely, when she was a partner at a London VC firm. It can be found on my website at: www.petercowley.org/lifelearnings

And so, I will finish this chapter with a different letter – a personal one to my late-teenage self.

Dear Peter,

You will go through tough times. Many will say that you've had more than your fair share of family deaths, health issues and business failures, but you've coped and been resilient.

Some lessons that you will need to learn are these:

You will be told many times that life is not a dress rehearsal and that you have only chance at it, so don't waste your life – grasp opportunities, contribute to others' lives, but also have time for yourself. Related to this is 'don't sweat the small stuff'. This is a bit hackneyed, but so important: life is full of priorities and the skill to work out what you want from life and hence making hourly/daily/yearly choices takes time to develop.

You were born into a family with a comfortable income, but lacking the ability to communicate emotionally, and it will take until your early forties to develop a level of emotional maturity. Read, and use professional help as soon as you can to build up and develop your emotional intelligence.

You'll never be worried about collecting assets or about your appearance. Stick with that programme, as experiences are much more valuable than assets. However, you should keep a better eye on your weight. You will reach your adult minimum weight in your mid-twenties and then you'll lose control of your weight for the following forty years. Although you will continue to play squash, you could easily have needed new hips or knees. Don't take forty-five years to learn how to enjoy running. Start now.

You have started to keep a personal diary. Please spend a few minutes a week maintaining this and it will make writing your memoirs a lot easier!

You will become a parent who feels they didn't spend enough time with their kids as they were growing up. Please make sure you do.

You will dislike speaking in public until your mid-fifties, when you will finally take Ian's counselling and learn to enjoy it. Start doing that now.

You won't prioritise reading novels. Try and allocate enough time to read at least one novel a month.

Personal relationships are key to a good life. You will have three marriages – two with a relationship of over seventeen years and one unlikely to last seventeen years unless you're lucky enough to be in the long tail of advanced cancer survivors.

You will adopt 'strong opinions, weakly held' in your late fifties. It will take that many decades to develop a big enough audience that your opinion is heard.

We all have and need stress in our lives, and you will learn to recognise that stress can be beneficial in avoiding procrastination. But you'll develop an intense addiction to alcohol to anaesthetise yourself from personal stresses and this could easily kill you. You will spend at least a decade in denial of this fact. Please face up to the reality that you have a problem as soon as you can.

And finally: good luck. Stick to your core values, never give up, help others, enjoy life and be kind to yourself.

Weblinks for reference

Some of Ian's poetry can be found on his memorial website at:
www.namgyal-essense.co.uk

Further information:
www.petercowley.org
www.investedinvestor.com

Cancer:
www.youtube.com/@project-cancer/videos
www.egfrpositive.org.uk
www.roycastle.org

Suicide and mental health:
www.papyrus-uk.org
www.centre33.org.uk

Addiction:
www.alcoholics-anonymous.org.uk

About the authors

PETER COWLEY is a serial entrepreneur and angel investor. He has founded and run a dozen businesses and has invested his own money in more than seventy-five startups. He was the President of the European Business Angel Network and UK Angel of the Year 2014. He has a degree from Cambridge University and an Honorary Doctorate from Anglia Ruskin University. He has mentored hundreds of entrepreneurs and been on the board of forty companies and a trustee of seven charities. Peter co-founded the Venture Capital company Martlet Capital. He was chair of the Cambridge Angels and is a Fellow in Entrepreneurship at the University of Cambridge Judge Business School. He was a non-executive director of the UK Business Angel Association and is on the investment committee of the UK Angel CoFund. He is a popular speaker and travels the world sharing his experiences, good and bad, with entrepreneurs and angel investors. With his late son, Alan, he has published eighty podcasts and two books for angel investors and entrepreneurs. He enjoys running, skiing and playing real tennis. He lives in Cambridge with his wife Liesbeth Blom.

LIESBETH BLOM was born in the Netherlands but has lived and worked in the UK for over thirty years. She has a PhD in Medieval English and is a freelance language consultant, translator, editor and occasional interpreter in both English and Dutch. While bringing up her family, she was active in the local community at both a grassroots and an organisational level, as a governor of a local school, chair of the Anglo-Dutch Society of Cambridge, President of the Cambridge University Musical Society Chorus and Editor of *Neerlandia* magazine. She is a keen singer, runner and fen skater. She lives in Cambridge with husband Peter Cowley.